DOGGY STYLE

"A hobby breeder's guide to achieving a safe, successful and stress-free dog pregnancy"

Sara Lamont

First Edition published 2022

A catalogue record for this book is available from The British Library

ISBN 978-1-3999-2317-0

www.caninefamilyplanner.com

To the best dog I 've ever bred, Lacey.

Champion LaRoyal 's Best Kept Secret JW
19/08/2011 - 2/12/2021

She was frigging exceptional.

I spent a quarter of my life with her, and don't I know it. She gave me so much fun, provided me with so many magical moments and memories, opened the door to many opportunities and gave me confidence in my abilities.

Is it possible a four-legged friend can provide so much and ask for such little in return? She made breed history, she's a legend, and will never ever be forgotten.

To me, she was the true epitome of dog showing fairness.Everything she won was on her own merit, and I thank all the judges that appreciated what she brought to the breed table.

She was a happy hound, always had a tail wag for anyone that would give her some attention. Neither of us knew that just hours after I last saw her, she'd pass surrounded by the few other LaRoyals I have. It was short and fast and though a shock for me, the best I could have asked for her.

Her legacy lives on through her progeny.

I can only feel it's the end of an era and the final chapter of what has been a transitional year.

RIP Superstar Lacey

Contents

What Breeders and Pet Professionals have said about Doggy Style

"Even if you are a moderately experienced breeder, you couldn't go far wrong reading this book just in case, as I'm sure many breeders will find something they haven't considered or experienced themselves yet. Despite having bred three litters and been around many experienced breeders in the showing community, many subjects were covered that hadn't crossed my mind or ears in anywhere near as much detail as I read in this book."

Ashley Ware - Discobull

"Read this informative book before you decide to breed, and certainly make sure you've read it before the birds and the bees bit takes place!!! This book will prepare you for what to do before you get anywhere near that stage (and will prepare you for that stage too - don't expect romance!). I feel that the book is full of gems. I will take a lot from it - I will be better cognisant of the costs involved and things that I can do to best facilitate a successful breeding experience."

Katie Duffy (Sussex)

"I know I would have done things differently had I read this book first. Some of the things I did before breeding and during pregnancy, I now understand the need for these steps. Having read this book, I feel a lot more knowledgeable about breeding… even when it doesn't always result in a pregnancy."

Liz O 'Hara - Rookhaugh

"It is a lovely read, really comprehensive. I can't fault it, congratulations once again."

Alex Selles Llorens, MRCVS - Medivet (Forest Row)

"A fun but realistic guide for the aspiring breeder."

Vicki Rushton - Jenberry

"Informative and enjoyable reading. Sections clearly outlined and thought for all aspects of breeding."

Helen Osborne-Brown - Perrymel

"I would describe it as 'very readable'. A touch of humour, some personal experiences, and a wealth of knowledge."

Michèle Jordan - Chocladorais

"A great source of information for any breeder or stud dog owner who's considering breeding from their dog. Easy to read and full of up to date information about everything you MUST know about dog breeding with a touch of humour thrown in. "

Sarah Malandrino - Altamont

"A very sensible book covering so many subjects beyond the normal whelping books available. Written by a lovely lady with a wealth of knowledge."

Lynne Stringer - Tumbledown

"This book is really knowledgeable if you would like to know more about breeding and how you go about it. This book is excellent and emphasises the need to better the breed. I am still making the good choices as I learn, but this book brought it home to me to make the right choices and why."

Tracy Williams (West Sussex)

"This book offers good information about sire and dam and their roles and the need for excellent health tests and ovulation tests. It also details the AI procedure, which has been interesting and would be less daunting if used next time."

Helen Hancox - Helkelbecian

"Facts without flannel, put in a simple to understand way."

Christine Sheppard - Carmiably

"No need to Google and search various information. This book has all you need to decide if to breed or not to breed."

Jana Griffin - Griffial

"Very informative, a really good read."

Tracey Coulman-Hole - Womlu

"A great little book that contains a lot of common sense, well worth reading if you contemplate breeding from your dogs."

Sue Badman - Tecklebridge

PREFACE

They say everyone has a book in them, I'm not going to lie, I can't believe I wrote a second. I had seemingly forgotten the early mornings, long days and late nights typing away at my PC with an extra bum pillow to stop it going numb. Trying to get the book finished outside my daily activities, chores and essentials whilst getting up in the dark and watching the winter evenings draw in fast.

In my first book, Not Born Yesterday (NBY), I specifically remember saying:

"You'll notice this book doesn't cover the "birds and the bees" of dog breeding, or like most 'breeding books', whether you should actually mate or not. For most people I see, the decision was made at least four weeks previous, or they might be dealing with an unintended or unknown pregnancy."

Yeah, about that…

This is the "birds and the bees" dog breeding book. Ultrasound scanning dogs for pregnancy is a large proportion of my work, and if the results are positive, I can suggest my previous book, NBY, to set them on their breeding journey. If the scan was negative, I had various bits of information to pass on, but nothing as comprehensive as this book.

The ideas were floating around in my head, and it was just a matter of getting pen to paper or fingers to keyboard.

What's happened since I published NBY? A house move, a pandemic and a few more litters. That's enough to keep anyone busy. I know the C-word invokes a reaction from most, but it sent the dog breeding world a little crazy from my perspective.

Any puppies of any quality were selling for crazy money. It was madness for a while, like shortages of freezers, pasta, toilet roll and petrol. You couldn't have guessed what the next hot item would be.

My fear is that many of these lockdown puppies with understandably questionable temperaments will be bred. I foresee the market becoming more flooded and anticipate stabilising in a few years, and some normality will be restored. I hope this book helps support dog owners to breed with the best intentions for their dogs, the puppies and the breed, rather than just their bank balance.

I feel now more than ever that you will need to stand out from the crowd to attract the new puppy owners you desire.

I started writing this book whilst rearing my 33rd litter, born in November 2020. Three pups were delivered by c-section, but still, such an easy litter that never lost weight and had the most attentive mum, Dusty. It meant that whilst feeding, I could start to collate the foundations of a possible book from my own online publications and client content I had already written.

The pups left at 8 weeks, and the partially written 20,000 word document gathered dust for a year.

Until Christmas 2021 that is. I decided I needed to finish the book before my next big birthday in February.

I've been really fortunate to have spent some key birthdays around the globe, my 30th in Las Vegas, my 25th in New York, my 18th in Florida and my 13th in Egypt.

Whilst in Egypt, my mother and I had visited Luxor with friends to check out the Valley of the Kings & Queens and the magnificent burial grounds of nobles from 1500-1070 B.C, including Tutankhamen. My mum organised a surprise party for me at the hotel, and guests even brought me gifts. We took a Felucca ride to Banana Island during Ramadan and were invited to eat with our hosts at dusk; these are still vivid memories for me.

I recall one tomb we visited was pretty modest from the outside, all things considered, and reasonably easy to access. It was small, cramped, dark and musty inside. Our hired travel guide stood outside and used a mirror to reflect sunlight into the tomb, so we could see the detailed and beautifully painted wall scriptures.

This book is the same for you. I'll shine the equivalent of an LED torch light into all the corners of breeding, even the dark ones, so you are best informed and enabled to make the correct decisions for you and your breeding dogs. But like my holiday guide with the mirror light, we may not entirely cover all topics in micro-detail with a magnifying glass, and you'll be left to do your own research if you find a topic of relevant interest.

So don't let me hold you up any further, let's get on with the show.

INTRODUCTION

I've worked as a Canine Family Planner™ since 2014. I'm not a Vet, I'm a pet professional that will show you the best practices when breeding in layman's terms, no technical talk here. If you want to learn long words to flex in front of friends, this book isn't for you. Equally, this isn't your book if you want a reference or textbook. There are enough veterinary written breeding books out there where you can get that kind of information.

This book is the real world, the actual reality of dog breeding. Dogs can't read, and at some point, you will get one that doesn't give a monkeys what a textbook says anyway. You'll need to use your own common sense and knowledge to do the best thing and make the right choices.

Unless you are born into a farming background surrounded by livestock, most people have relatively limited knowledge regarding animal reproduction.

Honestly, I caught an episode of Country File where a turkey was being 'manually manipulated' so the semen could be collected and many hens could be inseminated. It was enough to put you off your Christmas dinner.

I understand that it can feel challenging not knowing where to start with dog breeding, but this book will walk you through all the steps to ensure a successful and efficient canine conception.

The spectrum of the word 'breeder' is varied: Pet Breeder, Hobby Breeder, Home Breeder, I'm-not-a-Breeder, Show Breeder, One-time Breeder, Professional Breeder, Backyard Breeder and Greeder Breeder to name a few.

Getting people to agree on these definitions would be like a question from Family Fortunes, depending on your own perspective, principles and ethics, we all have differing opinions, benchmarks and expectations.

It's not my place to question your intentions to breed, there will be plenty of others more than forthcoming to judge. I hope it's done safely, with respect for the dogs, understanding of the breed, and appreciation of the responsibility you will have for any resulting puppies.

Regardless of which type of breeder you deem yourself to be, there can still be varying attitudes to breeding. This can span from the 'au naturel', letting nature take its course in every aspect and 'if it happens, it happens'. This optimism 'hopefully' results in puppies.

At the other end of the spectrum are breeders that will take advantage of every scientific or veterinary intervention to ensure breeding success, so puppies have the best chance of survival.

Despite pandemics and recessions, the pet industry is booming, alongside the continued evolution and advancement of breeding practices, techniques, and tools. Dog breeders tend to feel only the minor ripples when an economy slows, because people love their pets and view them as family. This typically means that they will often put their pet's needs above their own.

The practices in this book will help you increase your chances of breeding success, but they won't guarantee it. We all know the only thing guaranteed in this world are death and taxes.

You can do everything you should, but success can still escape you. It doesn't mean you're not a good owner or breeder. It means if you don't succeed try, try again. How many times you decide to try is up to you and your perseverance.

I've been through it myself with Tia, a female English Bulldog, bred at 18 months old she missed, we tried again 6 months later and she caught. Super stuff. She produced some beautiful puppies of which a keeper girl, Grace, won significantly at Crufts, the biggest dog show in the world.

We missed a year of seasons and bred her again for a second litter, which she missed. In fact, she missed three times to two different stud dogs. So on the fourth attempt, we put her back to the sire of the first litter, and she caught at 5.5yrs old. Jeeze.

You couldn't write it. She was ovulation tested on all breedings, so it seems she was only compatible with one suitor, her prince charming. The magic worked because she produced another top winning dog, Martin, who sired my breed record-breaking female called Lacey, to who I dedicated this book.

Tia's second litter was still not without complications, it was a litter of two pups born by c-section. She was taken very poorly after the operation due to blood clotting issues, and the puppies were hand-reared. I have no doubt if I knew then what I do now, she could have conceived on a much earlier attempt and probably could have avoided some of the later dramas.

Some owners can't cope with the disappointment of breeding, whilst others look at the experience and the financial loss and leave it be, and then you get the people that see it as a personal challenge.

I like the motto 'Nothing worth having comes easy' because, from my experience of dog breeding, it's true.

This book will uncover every relevant nook and cranny, setting you on a solid foundation for your breeding journey. It will reveal all relevant methods and techniques available, regardless of the dog and breed.

You might hear that "My breed doesn't do it like that" well then they are probably stuck in the dark ages, or the owners are at least. We all know many struggle to embrace the pace of change daily or personal, so why would breeding be any different?

Dog breeding isn't glamorous, mating rituals are weird, smelly and messy, and there aren't many mammals that look pretty whilst having sex. If you have been fortunate to have had a breed mentor, they would have forewarned and prepared you. If you haven't discovered such a rare gem on your travels, I promise this book will be the next best thing. I'll be honest with you and tell you what you do and don't want to hear.

The Power of 3

Three is a magic number
Yes it is, it's a magic number

Somewhere in that ancient mystic trinity
You get three as a magic number
The past and the present and the future
Faith and hope and charity
The heart and the brain and the body
Give you three as a magic number
It takes three legs to make a tripod or to make a table stand
It takes three wheels to make a vehicle called a tricycle
And every triangle has three corners
Every triangle has three sides
No more, no less, you don't have to guess
When it's three, you can see
It's a magic number

A man and a woman had a little baby
Yes, they did
They had three in the family
And that's a magic number

- Bob Dorough -

The number 3 is a unique number for the human brain because it's the smallest number we need to create a pattern. Patterns help us relate to the world around us, clearly highlighted in the famous song lyrics above.

This effect is powerful and has been fully harnessed by leaders and businesses. The pattern can be found in advertisements, speeches and any other message designed to have a persuasive effect. I'm not here to coax you, but I certainly want to create a structure that helps you remember some pretty useful information, otherwise, you wouldn't have bought this book.

"A man and a woman had a little baby, yes they did" this book has been written in three defined dog breeding sections. Part One is for the Bitch owner, focusing on preparing for such a breeding adventure.

Part Two is vital for any male dog owner considering offering their dog at public stud. The information will help you manage your male correctly, detailing how to conduct affairs and offer a reliable service.

Part Three is for both parties; this covers the available options to safely and successfully breed your dogs together.

Each section can be read independently, but if you want a comprehensive overview of dog breeding and how to avoid any potential pitfalls, I recommend you read all three parts.

If this is the first book you've read that I have authored, you are in for a treat. I can confidently say that no other dog breeding book is written in my style.

I'm not all about quoting facts and figures like a textbook. Yes, breeding is Biology; it's science, but that's what we have vets for, isn't it? They slog their guts out for seven years in vet school. Though I'm told canine reproduction makes up a tiny part of their syllabus (unless they specialise in that field), we've all probably had the conversation or possible lecture of getting your dog neutered on their first visit.

Breeding is not just a science but an art form, making you a creator of canines. Spending your time and effort to learn some basic skills will carry you far in understanding how and why to breed the best dogs possible. Approaching animal professionals, such as your vet, armed with such attitudes will ensure they recognise and respond to you appropriately.

A vet's worse nightmare is a naive, uneducated owner deciding they want to breed from their dog. The first question they will always ask is 'Why?'. In fact, it's the first question I also ask. We'll delve deep into Chapter One to answer this.

If you finish that chapter and still want to breed, this book will be worth its weight in gold. In fact, if you read the chapter and decide breeding isn't for you, then it's still been a worthy purchase and will save you much time, energy and emotions in the long run.

So let's crack on and get stuck into Part 1 - 'The Bitch'.

- PART ONE: The Bitch -

CHAPTER 1

Deciding to Breed

I moved into a new home whilst still in a very dilapidated state, just before rearing the litter that spurred me to write this book. I knew what I needed to accommodate the dogs and me when looking to buy. I opted for a 1960's bungalow as they have workable floorspace, which gives you more opportunity to reconfigure the floor plan.

I had the chimney removed, swapped the lounge into a bedroom (which was re-plastered), and then I put my magical interior decor touches on it. One room was nearly 90% finished.

And then it rained, hard.

Water started cascading through my newly plastered and painted window reveal. I sourced a tub to collect the rainwater and decided to investigate further when the weather had improved. Though I was new to the house, I knew it was a new problem because all the brick was dry previously.

I spoke to my neighbour who I shared the guttering with, and they acknowledged they had seen the overflowing guttering but had no leaks into their house. I then wondered if taking down the chimney was having an impact?

Fortunately, because I bought a bungalow, there are no serious heights involved with looking in the guttering, so I had a nosey. It was full of moss and silt. I cleared and cleaned my part, and then I realised that I might as well do my neighbours because it was shared. They are elderly and would never have managed themselves

- they certainly didn't refuse my offer. I removed nearly 12kg of debris.

Whilst I was at that height, I spied a crack in one of my roof tiles above the window.

I quickly called my 'builder minded' brother, and he suggested masticing the crack. The only one to hand was white bathroom sealant. He raised a valid point, just because the water is entering the house at a particular point, it might not actually be leaking from there as water has the freedom to travel easily.

And then I waited until it rained.

- Will the cleared guttering stop the overflow?
- Did removing the chimney cause the issue?
- Was the crack letting water in?

I made no assumptions that the first would work, I did all three 'fixes' hoping that one would rectify the issue.

And it rained… hard… again.

The guttering overflowed still, so that particular problem wasn't fixed. I went into the loft to see if any water was travelling on the beams. Nothing. That ruled out the chimney causing the issue.

The reveal remained dry, which suggested the problem had been identified, it was the cracked roof tile that could be easily replaced.

Breeding is the same. You need to follow a process of elimination to ensure your female can be bred. It shouldn't be the case of, Why not? Just because you own a female.

There are many avenues you should consider, and if after all that, you still want to, then fair enough. By then, you'll be fully aware of the bigger picture and the impact your actions will have.

Now I get it, everyone has to start breeding somewhere but make sure you start in the best possible position because it's impossible to reverse bad breeding. You can't rewind the clock and pretend some puppies that were substandard in health weren't born.

So please, consider all of the following reasons why you shouldn't breed before you actually do.

Breeding with Ethics

To breed or not to breed?

You probably shouldn't breed if:

- You think she will benefit from having a litter
- You just want another puppy
- Your female is not in good physical health
- Your female does not have a good temperament
- You don't have time to rear a litter
- You don't have the money to pay for associated breeding expenses
- You don't plan to breed the best puppies possible

I might be pointing out the obvious, and we'll cover all aspects of the above in this book, but let's first look at a concept called "Cognitive Dissonance". It's something I observe in Breeders all the time, so I thought I'd shed a little light on the phenomenon.

Breeding Cognitive Dissonance

The term Cognitive Dissonance is used to describe the mental discomfort that results from holding two conflicting beliefs, values or attitudes. This inconsistency between what people believe and how they behave motivates people to engage in actions that will help minimise feelings of discomfort. People attempt to relieve the tension in different ways, such as rejecting, explaining away or avoiding new information.

For example, if I was to mention tax implications to someone I had just scanned with their female in pup, the majority would very quickly tell me they don't breed for money, they aren't a 'breeder' as such and that they don't make any substantial profit. Yet the majority don't keep any form of accounts to know if this is the truth. Any profit over £1,000 is taxable and pretty easy to achieve in some breeds.

There are many ways cognitive dissonance can trigger mental conflict. Forced Compliance is when you find yourself engaging in behaviours that are opposed to your own beliefs due to external expectations, including going along with something due to peer pressure.

Sometimes learning new information can lead to cognitive dissonance, or you engage in a behaviour that you later learn is harmful. People try to justify the behaviour or find ways to discredit or ignore the information to deal with this. The "back-to-back" breeding discussion may fall into this category, which I will cover later in this book.

Decision making can also cause cognitive dissonance, and people begin to justify their choice as they believe they made the right decision. Possibly when explaining why you picked a particular stud dog, even though he's not ticked some of your basic requirements of health testing or temperament, and then produces puppies with similar traits or issues.

This is an example I recently witnessed. A breeder imports a male puppy for their breeding program. A costly option, around £15,000. The male puppy grows, and he only has one descended testicle (Cryptorchidism). They are naturally really disappointed. They have two conflicting views, we've invested a lot of money, time and effort into importing and rearing this dog, and he has a very significant reproduction fault. But he was bought specifically for the breeding advancement of their bloodline.

So the breeder carries out a full DNA testing panel; the dog is of a suitable breed type and has a sound temperament. Hip and elbow scores are sufficient, and he's been fertility tested. All is good. So why did the breeder do this? To smooth the space in their mind between their two conflicting views. They have now managed to justify that the dog is of breeding merit and quality and could be used in their program.

In economics, there is the "Sunken Cost Fallacy" theory, our tendency as humans is to follow through on an endeavour if we have already invested time, effort and money into it, whether or not the current costs outweigh the benefits.

At this point, you can start to observe the differences between breeders. Some will do as I've mentioned, even if restricting the use of the dog for their own breeding plans. Others will cut their losses, understand the bigger picture of their breeding goals, and realise how a dog like this may cause irreparable long-term issues.

Ethical Breeding

From my experience 'on the road' offering dog breeding services to my clients, some owners tend to bend reality to fit their own truth. They can struggle to step back and objectively look at their actions and admit their primary motivations or are concerned about how others might view them.

For instance, there is a huge stigma about saying you breed dogs for money in the U.K. So much so that about 90% of my clients confirm they aren't by verbalising it. I personally don't have any issues with anyone breeding dogs and producing a high number of puppies, as long as they are of the best quality possible and finding quality homes. Breeding dogs is hard, it can be hit and miss unless you have many breeding bitches to provide a consistent income.

I know some will shudder at the thought, but what's the issue if the dogs are well cared for and loved?

The issue is how dog breeding has evolved over the decades.

The breeding licence was introduced by the Animal Welfare (England) Regulations in 2018. Its purpose was to clarify the required husbandry that should be achieved when breeding dogs, whilst creating a widely recognised star grading benchmark for future puppy owners to identify good breeders.

I feel the introduction of this licence, although in principle seems a good idea, has been highly disappointing. Local governments have interpreted the legislation differently, meaning the application of breeder grading has been inconsistently managed across the varying counties. Such inadequacy is detrimental to the licence structure and means confidence is lost in its purpose and implementation.

The legislation also fails to recognise (because it's supported by DEFRA, which is concerned about the commercial entity of food and agricultural affairs) the difference between high-level commercial dog breeders and people who are 'home breeders'. By virtue, all breeders are channelled through the same process, assessment and reviewed as commercially focused dog breeders. Which, in my opinion, is inappropriate, and instead, the process should be seeking to correctly define, highlight and encourage the difference.

The Kennel Club attempted something similar with the Assured Breeders Scheme for Pedigree dogs, but there is a myriad of crossbreeds, designer dogs and independent registries that the Kennel Club doesn't cover.

The American author and philosopher Aldo Leopold once said;

"Ethical behaviour is doing the right thing when no one else is watching — even when doing the wrong thing is legal."

I think Aldo has summed this up perfectly.

All your dog breeding actions should be because it's the right thing to do for the dog, not because that's acceptable or expected.

Chapter 1 - Deciding to Breed summary

During this chapter, we have covered:

- The importance of breeding dogs ethically, and to the highest possible standards and schemes available.
- Acknowledging when you are experiencing cognitive dissonance and how that may impact your breeding decisions and behaviours.
- Contemplating if the level of dedication and commitment for dog breeding is suitable for you and accepting that it may not suit you.

Let's consider your breeding purpose and personal aims in the next chapter.

CHAPTER 2

What's your Breeding Purpose

Do you want another puppy?

I'm a show breeder and proud of it, but I serve many different types of breeders in my business, and it's not for me to judge them. With that in mind, there's not a bat in hells chance I would breed if I didn't show, well certainly not English Bulldogs anyway.

I breed because I want to keep the best puppy of the litter, which I plan to exhibit as they grow and, if I've done an outstanding job, will hopefully become a breed champion. I'm not even a competitive person, but I love the sense of a personal challenge and accomplishment of imagining something into existence. The idea of picking a stud, breeding the dogs, and then rearing the puppies is hopefully a direct reflection of the vision I had in my mind.

It's even better to be recognised for your hard efforts by peers, and hopefully, that will go someway [for me] to ticking the box, that I've achieved something in my life.

More so for my achievements to be collectively observed and acknowledged by peers who felt I had left the breed better than I found it. One day, I'll hope to be the one-minute silence of remembrance and respect at the start of a breed show. Or maybe that my Bulldog memorabilia collection will get auctioned for a profit for a breed club, or even that people just remember my dogs, more than me, fondly reminiscing on the amazingly consistent features, breed type or health they had.

If I didn't want all of the above, I would just buy a puppy if I wanted another one. Too much hard work, heartache, and sleepless nights make it worth any other option. It's probably also a less monetary risk to buy a puppy in some breeds than to breed one.

We just want her to have a litter

I'm always slightly miffed when people state, "We just want her to have one litter".

I don't believe any female dog has ever desired to be a mother, they aren't aware of their biological clock. Yes, they may be super flirty when in season, but that's hormones, nothing more. She never sits and wonders what her kids might look like, whether any of her pups will make the grade as a bomb detection dog or guide dog. The main person in her relationship should be you, the human that cares for her and the broader family that looks after her.

The humanisation of animals, particularly dogs, seems to be only growing. It's not all bad; it certainly shows a mark of the owner's respect, prestige and the importance of a pet being in their life.

Where is the line of acceptability?

In yesteryear, dogs served specific roles working for us, retrieving, hunting, herding or guarding, of course, some still do. Nowadays, the roles are more varied, including therapy, assistance, protection and companion dogs.

Many people have hobbies associated with their dogs, whether that be exhibition, agility, canicross, sledging, competitive grooming… and that just scratches the surface.

They can also be a huge source of entertainment, you only have to scroll through YouTube videos, Facebook memes and Instagram images. Not to mention the doggy boutiques and couture dog clothes, prams and customised birthday cakes available these days.

What's my point?

If you breed a litter, the only person that 'wants' this is you.

That's fine, but don't be deluded that you're doing it for any other reason, even if you own a rare breed that your registries encourage you to breed. They still can't force you. Your dog will have a litter because you want her to, not because she wants to. She'll carry pups, deliver and rear them, all because you wanted her to.

In doing so, you are signing up for more than just rearing a litter of puppies; you need to consider what ongoing support you can offer after the initial sale of the puppy. What efforts did you make to avoid any severe or hereditary health conditions? Are you aware of your breed's ailments to prevent breeding them in the first place?

To a degree, it doesn't matter where you sit on the dog breeder spectrum, as long as you understand your intention to breed and that fits comfortably with your expectations and values as a person.

You need to consider your breeding aims; otherwise, it will most likely become challenging to make the right choices. I'll share mine:

A. Breed the healthiest, well-adjusted puppy possible
B. Breed a puppy that is the epitome of its breed

Because health and breed type is important to me, I don't cost puppies in a litter differently because I put the same effort into all the puppies when I rear a litter. It's my job to match each puppy to its perfect owner.

When you think about the importance of placing a puppy, it shouldn't be on markings or colour. It should be on the puppy's personality, temperament, lifestyle, and purpose for the owner. Managing these requirements helps keep dogs out of rescue shelters or breed charities.

Even when you try to breed the best and healthiest puppies, they are still a bundle of biology. Sometimes even with all the possible parent health testing, some puppies may develop unforeseen health conditions, and you'll have to manage this. With this in mind, in the next chapter, we'll look at the available health testing and schemes for any breed of dog. Before that, check out the article I found online (below).

Breeding for Profit

Illegal bulldog breeders PosherBulls fined £450,000

A MARRIED couple who raked in a fortune by illegally breeding and selling bulldogs have been ordered to pay more than £450,000 of it back.

PosherBulls run from a four-bedroom detached home in Bonvilston, Vale of Glamorgan, the couple pleaded guilty to charges under the Animal Welfare Act 2006.

The pair, who have three children, admitted not having an appropriate licence and failing to meet the needs of the dogs in their care, including forcing bitches to undergo multiple pregnancies and deliver more than one litter a year.

Husband and wife team were not giving their breeding dogs enough time to recover, often artificially inseminating them soon after they had given birth to a previous litter, Cardiff Crown Court was told.

In January 2018, they were told if they had another litter of puppies they would need a breeding licence, with failure to obtain one possibly leading to prosecution.

Despite being told multiple times, they chose not to apply for one and a vet later concluded that, had an application been submitted, it would not have been successful.

After an investigation by the Shared Regulatory Services (SRS) on behalf of Vale of Glamorgan Council, a warrant was executed in December 2019 at the couple's home, where 28 dogs were found in outbuildings.

At another of the properties in the village, officers found a further 24 dogs, while another six dogs were found at a third property in

North Cornelly.

The couple bred at least 67 litters between 2014 and 2020, it was revealed.

Information on known carried out C-sections indicated 43 of those litters were delivered in one year alone between 2018 and 2019.

One dog, Coco, had six litters within a four-year period while numerous others were forced to deliver two litters in less than a 12-month period.

Their dog were registered with five different veterinary practices and litters were given different names and addresses to avoid detection by both the local authority and Kennel Club, the court was told.

Investigations under the Proceeds of Crime Act revealed they made £372,531 from the illegal business, but had available assets of more than £1 million.

www.southwalesargus.co.uk

12/1/2022

Is there much more I need to stay?

Now don't get me wrong, people make money breeding dogs, whether they care to admit it or not. The majority of these same people most probably spend a large majority of that money back on the dogs and their welfare. However, some do not, as demonstrated above; some also neglect the dogs in the process. The whole purpose of this book and my other, Not Born Yesterday, is to make sure breeders are educated to understand the boundaries of these conflicting issues and to act accordingly and appropriately.

If you decide to breed for a significant profit, you'll need to meet any obligations that come with the decision. You'll be required to keep and submit annual financial accounts. Registries such as the Kennel Club will require evidence of a Breeding Licence when you register more than three litters in a rolling year. The Breeding Licence also has strict requirements and is legislation heavy with enforcing the conditions of how dogs should be kept, managed and bred.

Once assessed for a council Breeding Licence and if approved, you'll be advised on how many litters you can breed annually and how many dogs can be kept in a household. This is typically restricted to a reasonable number for a residential home. Any large scale would most likely need planning permission for change of use for the property and subject to its own further scrutiny. Therefore, most of the time, the limit is set similar to the Kennel Clubs restrictions.

Who should or shouldn't apply for a breeding licence is still very much a grey area. Relevant factors include how you advertise your puppies, the frequency of puppy sales and the prices they are being sold for. Posherbulls should have held a licence, but in doing so, it would have forced them to comply with practices that weren't beneficial for their business, such as back-to-back breedings.

If you decide a breeding license isn't for you, I recommend that any breeder, on any scale, should keep good financial records for their activities. Without these details, you'll struggle to argue otherwise with any authorities on your breeding conduct or management, should you be reviewed or investigated.

Chapter 2 - Breeding Purpose summary

During this chapter, we have covered:

- The benefits of how identifying your breeding purpose and subsequent goals will aid your breeding choices.
- Having a defined breeding purpose will help you make suitable and relevant breeding practices and stud selection choices.
- The Breeding requirements and legislation should you decide to breed frequently.

CHAPTER 3

Breeding Health

So, you've still decided to breed? What's considered good health?

I can share with you that, sadly, I've ultrasound scanned dogs and confirmed pregnancy when I can visually see the dog has terrible eyes or felt a slipping knee cap or popping hip joint, and as I keep saying, I'm no vet.

These girls shouldn't have been bred; they are not in their best physical condition. Not to mention that some of these conditions are hereditary, so they will be passed to their puppies. Meaning they could develop similar issues of living in discomfort and pain and, worse, be life-limiting.

If the owners had taken the time to take them to a vet and find this out, they might have considered whether it was the right thing for them to do, which is why they probably never took them.

Denying the truth doesn't change the facts, yes you might be lucky, and only a few of the puppies carry that same DNA, and only time will tell if, as they grow, it too becomes a problem for them.

I'll refer to the cognitive dissonance theory; what story are you telling yourself that your decision is the best option? When breeding, you need to objectively judge, looking at the presented facts rather than using feelings and opinions.

But is it fair to the new puppy owners?

Do you want to deal with this kind of expectation, disappointment, and, possibly worse, a court case? I've known puppy buyers take breeders to court over dogs suffering life-limiting conditions. Then you maybe be asked to present evidence of what you did as a breeder to avoid any severe long-term conditions. What will you show them?

This is one of the reasons why health screening is so important. It could save you a lot of aggravation in the long term.

The fact that you've never taken your dog to the vet, or that your vet has given her the thumbs up for her general health and condition is not enough evidence. There are more in-depth checks available.

You'll need to research what's available for your particular breed. If you have a crossbreed or a designer dog, you may have to conduct tests for all the main breeds. Considering the implications of a dog's DNA results, there are other equally important factors to consider when deciding whether two dogs should be mated together, such as temperament, genetic diversity, available health tests and the general conformation of the dogs. Your breeding decisions should always be well balanced and consider the qualities and compatibility of the sire and dam you are mating.

Vet Health Check

A basic vet-check is not enough to approve a dog for breeding.

A veterinary health check consultation is an opportunity for the vet to check the animal's welfare and probe about any changes that the owner may not have noticed, such as behaviour, drinking, eating, sleeping, and toileting. And discuss preventative care such as vaccines, worming and fleas. They also check for dental health and weight, looking at historical visit information for any noticeable changes. They will carry out a 'nose to tail' examination to check the eyes, ears, teeth, coat and limbs, listen to the heart and lungs, palpate the abdomen, and check the temperature with an opportunity for the owner to ask questions.

This type of check is an 'as seen' observation, it will not tell you about the female's breeding ability, potential or capacity to produce healthy puppies. 99% of the time, if you mention breeding to the vet, they are likely to suggest spaying as the best option. They are unlikely to give you much support on what you can do to ensure your female is in the best condition to be bred from, advise on genetic testing to avoid hereditary diseases, or how to seek a suitable stud dog.

That is undoubtedly down to you, so this book will be one of the best places to start.

Breed Clubs & Health Schemes

Breed clubs are typically run by voluntarily elected committees of people who own or are interested in the breed. Their purpose is to protect the breed by supporting and educating new and existing owners and breeders on the health and welfare of the breed. They highlight good ethics and encourage dog owners to follow basic principles to maintain a suitable standard of behaviour within the breed. Helping to support and guide owners through various activities, including dog shows and educational seminars.

Breed clubs exist for all Kennel Club (KC) recognised breeds and may be regional or national. If there are numerous Breed Clubs for a breed, they may all report to a national Breed Council, which then liaises between the registry, such as the KC and the clubs. Breeds under alternative registries are also forming Breed Clubs to help bridge this communication gap and help support owners.

Breed clubs often have recognised 'Health Schemes' and maintain reports, asking owners to provide evidence of their dog's health testing results to consolidate this information which then can be researched to help better the breed.

They may issue recognition certificates typically following a Gold, Silver, or Bronze structure that the owner/breeder can promote and share. This is a recognisable way for stud dogs to share their health status with bitch owners and breeders to share the health status of the puppies' parents with new owners.

Some stud owners may have minimum health requirements for any bitches put to their dogs. If the bitch is tested with a registry approved DNA Laboratory, copies of the results may be stored directly on their system. This information is in the public domain and can be found for research and interest. For example, you've enquired about using a particular stud dog. You can then check for compatibility on a system called MyKC for Kennel Club registered dogs without contacting the owner directly.

The breed clubs may ask for similar health information, but they will collate the data to create an overall 'league' table of data with all the tested dogs and their achievements. It would still be down to the owners to ask for copies of the certificates to check for themselves.

Laboratories such as Embark run multiple DNA panels providing breed insight, health and ancestry for each dog on an online profile. The owner can decide what information is publicly accessible and encourages the uploading of further health certificates. This online profile can be easily shared and researched as required by any proactive dog breeder.

Physical Health Screening

Let's look closer at some of the required assessments or tests deemed relevant and beneficial when breeding dogs.

Hip & Elbow dysplasia screening scheme by the British Veterinary Association (BVA/KC)- Dysplasia is a complex inherited condition where the joint does not develop correctly. As a dog gets older, the joint undergoes wear and tear and deteriorates, leading to a loss of function.

This can cause varying degrees of pain, discomfort, stiffness and lameness. The most reliable way of determining the health of a dog's hip or elbows is by having your dog X-rayed locally and assessed by a specialist panel once submitted.

The X-ray will be taken under anaesthesia or sedation. Your dog's results can then be sent to the BVA/KC scheme for grading. The score can be compared to the breed median, allowing breeders to make informed breeding decisions.

The scheme is open to all dogs, including crossbreeds, unrecognised breeds, and dogs not registered with the Kennel Club. This information will help you confirm if the dog is suitable for a breeding program.

For example, the BVA data shows over 15 years, the English Bulldog has an average score of 40.0 from 31 tested dogs, and the Labrador has a much lower average score of 11.3 from over 50,000 dogs. Numerous facts need to be taken into account than just the data alone. How large is the tested pool, and why? Along with considering the breed's purpose and conformation.

It's generally agreed (but numbers will depend on the breed) that you want a hip score to be as low as possible and the numbers across both hips to be as even as obtainable. For example, 3:3 is better than a 0:6, even though they both total 6.

For most breeds, elbows are required to be 0:0, but for instance, an English Mastiff (considered a vulnerable breed) above 0 would still be acceptable to breed.

At a quick glance, the BVA data does include many breeds Boerboels, Cockapoos, Golden and Labradoodles, so it's certainly worth casting your eye over. I also wanted to include alternative views to hip and elbow scoring.

PupScan

PupScan is pioneering an alternative view of the older method of X-raying. Founded in 2015 and supported by specialist orthopaedic consultants both in veterinary and human medicine, the project investigates the life events that result in the development of joints, particularly in hips and elbows. They are looking to find the baseline, which may vary from breed to breed, to establish normal joint development as early in life as possible.

They are offering a Puppy Screening service where puppies in a litter from 8 to 12 weeks old can have their joints ultrasound scanned which is a non-invasive and low stress. This data will help them identify if dysplasia is hereditary or environmental and be able to educate breeders on how to reduce hip issues for puppies in the whelping box.

PupScan believes that each breed will most likely need its own hip grading score rather than X-ray scoring with no diagnosis. A condition diagnosis will also help identify if the issue has been caused due to the environment, such as poor husbandry, including insufficient bedding and slippery floors. If so, these dogs should not be excluded from the breeding gene pool, as it's not a hereditary form that would pass to offspring.

PupScan is keen to hear from any owners who have females confirmed in pup and wish to participate in this study; full details are at www.thepupscanproject.co.uk.

Heart scheme (KC)- This scheme applies to all breeds, advising owners if their dog is affected by heart disease, providing guidance to breeders on lowering the risk of producing affected puppies. Several approved cardiologists (vets specially trained in heart conditions), have been appointed to carry out heart grading on dogs.

Breed clubs tend to have health sub-committees to educate, promote and share specific relevant testing for their breed. For instance, the Great Dane Breed Council collated from the Kennel Club Survey that nearly a quarter of Dane deaths were from Dilated Cardiomyopathy (DCM). With funding from the KC Charitable Trust, the club is researching the condition. Any suffering dogs can wear an echo-halter monitor for a day to help gather data. Combined with a simple blood test (to identify the cardiac biomarker), they hope to correctly identify and diagnose DCM. Allowing breeders to actively breed away from the condition, improving the breed's future.

Eye screening scheme (BVA/KC)- How an eye condition is inherited varies dramatically. Some eye conditions may be controlled by several different genes and environmental factors. Others may be entirely governed by just one gene, and some may not be inherited at all.

This scheme offers breeders the opportunity to screen for inherited eye disease by examining the eye. The eye scheme is not limited to identifying inherited eye disease but also includes a general assessment of the health of the eye and adnexa (eyelids, tear ducts and other parts around the eyeball).

Adult dogs should be examined under the eye scheme before being used for breeding. This should be carried out repeatedly and regularly, within 12 months before mating; especially in the breeds where inherited eye disease can develop later in life.

For breeds with an inherited eye disease that can be detected soon after birth (congenital and neonatal disease), screening puppies as part of a litter is usually between 6 and 12 weeks of age.

Gonioscopy with BVA, KC, and International Sheep Dog Society (ISDS)- This eye exam looks for signs that a dog is affected by a painful and blinding disease known as primary glaucoma. Breeds at risk include but are not limited to: the Basset Hound, Dandie Dinmont, Japanese Shiba Inu, Leonberger, Retriever (Flat-Coated), Siberian Husky, Spaniel (American Cocker, Cocker, English Springer, Welsh Springer) and Spanish Water Dog.

The extent to which the eye is affected is recorded and given as a grade. This grade can be used to make health-focused breeding decisions that reduce the risk of producing puppies that grow up to be affected.

Deafness (BAER testing)- Deafness at birth (known as congenital deafness) is often inherited in breeds such as Dalmatians, English Setters, Border Collies, Australian Shepherds, White Boxers and White Bull Terriers.

This inherited condition is not fully understood but is believed to be controlled by many different genes, plus possibly by additional breed-specific risk factors.

The best age to test a litter is around 5.5 to 6.5 weeks, as the ear canals don't open until puppies are about 2 weeks old. The test can be carried out at any age after this, including on adult dogs. Many breeders wish to know the hearing status of their pups before picking their keeper puppy and before they leave for their new homes. Some mobile professionals offer this service, so you don't need to haul a large litter around for testing, but advance booking is needed.

Dogs not tested as a puppy should be tested before being considered for breeding.

Respiratory Function Grading Scheme (KC and the University of Cambridge)- The Respiratory Function Grading Scheme assesses Bulldogs, French Bulldogs and Pugs for a breathing problem known as BOAS (brachycephalic obstructive airway syndrome).

The scheme advises owners if their dog is affected by BOAS and gives guidance to breeders on how to lower the risk of producing affected puppies. A selection of regionally approved assessors (vets trained specially in BOAS) has been appointed to carry out respiratory function grading on dogs of these breeds and listed on the relevant breed club websites.

CM/SM screening scheme (BVA/KC) primarily examines toy breeds such as Affenpinschers, Cavalier King Charles Spaniels, Chihuahuas, Griffon Bruxellois, Havanese, Maltese, Papillons, Pomeranians, Yorkshire Terriers, but it is open to all dogs. Chiari-like malformation (CM) is a fault in the development of the skull, causing part of the brain to protrude from the opening at the back of the skull.

Syringomyelia (SM) refers to the presence of one or more fluid-filled pockets that may develop in the spinal cord, called syrinxes. CM/SM Scheme requires an MRI scan to identify signs of how a dog may be affected.

Physical Conformation - A dog's conformation refers to its overall structure and appearance. Dogs come in many different shapes and sizes. Having such varied conformation is one of the many fascinating things about dogs.

An example of health problems related to the exaggeration of physical conformation would be excessive skin, extreme head shapes, extremely flat faces, prominent eyes, tight or inverted tails, excessively long ears, or a large amount of hair in and around them.

The KC introduced 'Breed Watch' as an early warning system to identify points of concern for individual breeds. The aim is to provide information to dog show judges, breeders and exhibitors on visible health concerns to discourage the breeding of dogs with exaggerated conformational issues that are detrimental to the health and welfare.

It's split into three categories (that magic number again). Category 3 is considered 'high profile' breeds as they are more susceptible to developing eyes, skin, dentition, movement, and breathing problems. These include the Bloodhound, Bulldog, Dogue de Bordeaux, German Shepherd Dog, Mastiff, Neapolitan Mastiff, Pekingese, Pug and St. Bernard.

These breeds have to pass an independent veterinary health check looking for these particular issues to be awarded Best of Breed at Championship shows or obtain their Champion titles.

No vet checks are required for category 2, but the judges must report any points of concern to the KC for monitoring. This could result in the breed moving up or down in the category.

If the breed is in category 1, they have no current Breed Watch points of concern, but judges have the option to report any problems they see to the KC.

For the breed to move to a lower category, the Breed Clubs and councils have to work their arses off (in my words) to provide mountains of documented data to prove the KC otherwise. These sub-committees are unsung heroes of some breeds, and only a tiny number have managed to downgrade.

DNA Testing

DNA tests allow you to better understand your dog's genetics. These tests can inform you if your dog is likely to be affected by a specific condition or whether they may pass on the genes associated with these conditions if they're bred.

A dog's genetic material contains 2.8 billion base pairs of DNA. A 'gene' is a section of DNA with specific instructions for making a particular molecule. Each dog has two copies of every gene, one inherited from its dam and one from its sire.

These two genes may be the same or slightly different. These differing genes contribute to each puppy's unique physical features and account for the differences between each dog and breed.

Any dog can inherit a faulty gene, and this error, in turn, can be passed on to their puppies. The gene may have become faulty for many reasons, too many for this book, but the sheer act of DNA replication can cause an error.

Just like an incorrectly copied recipe, the impact it can have will depend on the type of error made. A spelling mistake of a common ingredient in a recipe may have no effect on the final meal while changing a cooking time could have severe consequences. Similarly, a mutant gene may have no apparent impact, or it could cause a severe health problem.

Congenital abnormalities or birth defects are conditions an animal is born with. Some of these conditions are inherited and occur within particular families or breeds, while others are caused by environmental factors such as chemicals, nutrition or injury during pregnancy. It's often difficult to identify the exact causes.

If the dogs you breed are prone to preventable health conditions, then the necessary health checks, tests, and supplements should be adhered to reduce the re-occurrence. The attitude of a breeder should be proactive in wanting to breed healthy dogs; this may require testing and screening before breeding, not once a problem has been discovered.

Autosomal Recessive Traits

An autosomal recessive disorder means two copies of an abnormal gene must be present for the disease or trait to develop.

If a puppy is born to parents who both carry the same autosomal recessive gene, they have a 1 in 4 chance of inheriting the abnormal gene from both parents and developing the disease. They have a 50% (1 in 2) chance of inheriting one abnormal gene. This would make them a carrier. A carrier is an individual who carries and is capable of passing on a genetic mutation associated with a disease and may or may not display disease symptoms.

In other words, for puppies born to parents who both carry the gene (but do not have signs of disease), the expected outcome for each puppy is:

- There is a 25% chance that the puppy is born with two normal genes (clear).
- There is a 50% chance that the puppy is born with one normal and one abnormal gene (carrier, without disease), the same as the parents.
- There is a 25% chance that the puppy is born with two abnormal genes (referred to as affected and is at risk for the disease).

Please remember that these outcomes do not mean that the puppy will definitely be carriers or be severely affected. Popular tests for such genetic disease include, but are not limited to:

- **Forms of Eye disease**
    - Progressive Retinal Atrophy (prcd-PRA)
    - Primary Lens Luxation (PLL)
    - Canine Multi-Focal Retinopathy (CMR 1/2/3)

    - o Glaucoma and Goniodysgenesis (GGD)
- **Forms of Kidney/Bladder disorders**
    - o Hyperuricosuria / Urate Stones (HUU, SLC)
    - o Cystinuria
    - o Polycystic Kidney Disease (PKD)
- **Other diseases**
    - o Larynx / Laryngeal Paralysis (LP) is a breathing disorder
    - o PK Deficiency (Pyruvate Kinase Deficiency) is a form of blood disorder

Coat colour

You'll need to conduct your own research to determine the most applicable tests for your breed. Some testing panels also include coat type and colour testing. Merle is also known as Dapple or Harlequin (depending on the breed). It's a particular coat pattern that has become seemingly popular over the last decade.

The Merle gene creates mottle patches of colour in a solid or piebald coat and impacts eye colour and skin pigment. The Merle gene has been introduced into breeds to which it wasn't native, meaning some breeders are not fully aware of the issues and repercussions that surround it. The merle colour issue is relevant to the following breeds (but the list may not be exhaustive): American Cocker Spaniel, Australian Shepherd, Border Collie, Cardigan Welsh Corgi, Chihuahua, Dachshund, Old English Sheepdog (Bobtail), English Bulldog, French Bulldog, Great Dane, Shetland Sheepdog (Sheltie), Rough Collie, Smooth Collie, Pomeranian, Pyrenean Shepherd, American Staffordshire Terrier, Hungarian Mudi, Catahoula Leopard Dog, Norwegian Dunker, Beauceron, and the Bergamasco.

The research is continually developing and expanding; currently, you can specifically test for the type of Merle pattern displayed in the coat, Harlequin(Mh), Atypical(Ma) and Cryptic (Mc). Merle is the only coat colour that can be directly detrimental to the dog itself. Puppies that are 'double Merle' in DNA have two copies of the dominant Merle allele (part of the DNA gene) expressed as 'M/M'(while a non-dominant recessive allele would be represented at 'm'). These dogs are mainly white-coated, with several possible health issues, including deafness and blindness. For this reason, two Merle's cannot be bred together; Merle dogs should only be bred to non-Merle/solid colours.

However, Cryptic or Phantom Merle dogs (Mc and Ma), may not visually appear to be Merle, but they carry the Merle gene. They would have been a product of a Merle breeding litter and consequently carry the gene from a parent but do not show Merle noticeably in their coat colour. For this reason, all dogs produced from a Merle breeding should be coat colour DNA tested before being bred, so their status is identified.

An invisible Merle is when the dog carries the Merle allele 'M', but it cannot be visually seen as it is masked by the dog's coat which is yellow, red, sable, fawn, gold or cream, so the Merle becomes invisible to the eye due to how it's expressed in the pigment. This would only be detected if tested.

See table overleaf of the varying Merle coat DNA combinations.

M/M M/Mc M/Ma M/Mh *(Or any combination of)*	Double Merle Merle/Cryptic Merle/Atypical Merle/Harlequin	The dog carries **two variants** of the dominant "M" allele. The dog is considered an affected "double Merle" because M/M dogs can be affected by deafness and ocular defects. M/M dogs will always pass on a copy of Merle to their offspring and should not be bred from.
m/M m/Mc m/Ma m/Mh	Merle Cryptic Atypical Harlequin	The dog has one copy of the "M" Merle allele and one negative "m" copy of the Merle allele. The dog can pass either allele on to any offspring. Not always seen as a visual Merle but "carries" the gene.
m/m	Non-merle	The dog has two copies of the recessive "m" allele and is negative for Merle. The dog will always pass on a negative copy of the Merle allele to all offspring. These are the only types of coat that should be bred to any other Merle carriers on this table.

Some registries will refuse registrations of Merle coated puppies that are not naturally occurring in the breed due to the associated health issues. However, breeders have been known to lie when registering the puppies, so it's still possible for a Merle to hold registration papers and the coat pattern to be incorrectly noted. Without DNA testing, you will never truly know.

Many Laboratories are offering canine DNA testing, some overseas offering better value. This can slow the results due to the international postage, but due to the DNA being collected via a mouth swab and suspended in a solution, the genetic material is not compromised. Popular U.K Labs include Weatherbys associated with the Kennel Club, Laboklin and Animal DNA Diagnostics and internationally, Embark.

Visit **www.caninefamilyplanner.com/embark** for a new breeder discount on your first DNA kit order.

Heritage Testing

Also for consideration is heritage testing which may be included in some DNA panels or an individual test with a brand like Wisdom Panel. These are particularly important for new and popular designer dogs such as Cockapoos, Labradoodles and Cavapoos.

A 100% pedigree dog would be considered at 'P Generation', e.g. a Labrador, Pug or Bullmastiff. 'F1 generation' is when one of the parents is a different purebred from the other; for example, a Labrador is bred to a Poodle, and the puppies will be F1 Labradoodles. 'F1' breedings typically produce the expected type of this breeding combination.

An 'F1b' generation is when one of the parents is F1 (50% P + 50% P) and the other a purebred (P); for example, a Labradoodle (F1) is bred to a Poodle (P), the puppies will be 75% P and 25% F1, this breeding will intensify traits in favour of the pedigree (P) parent.

An 'F2' generation is when two F1 parents are bred, Labradoodle (F1) and Labradoodle (F1). This type of breeding generates a higher variation between the puppies when it comes to size, colouration or coat type meaning the litter may lack consistency.

The most consistent breedings will be F1 or F1b. There are further generational breeding combinations like F2b, F3 and Multi-generation, which you can easily research online.

Mental Health

What 's considered a good temperament?

I'm asked many questions in my day to day role, one that always stands out and sticks in my head is, "Have you ever been bitten by a dog whilst working?"

The short answer is yes, but not by a female. I would have concerns about an owner breeding an aggressive female. Now, I have experienced some females that are a bit anxious or fearful, and yes, that could easily manifest to biting when combined with being super hormonal whilst in season. If you understand canine body language, it will provide many signs when a dog is uncomfortable. Side eye, licking lips, hackles, avoidance, hunching, the list can go on before they choose to growl and finally bite.

In fact, the dog I was bitten by didn't do any of these signs, hence I was caught out after being with him for nearly 45 minutes before he decided to bite, but that's another story.

Temperament is a dog's personality, makeup, or disposition which is genetic in dogs. This means dogs with poor temperaments should not be bred, male or female. This isn't just a dog showing aggression. Other signs displayed may include possessiveness or selfishness, typically over toys, food or reacting due to fear.

Temperament is about how a dog reacts to certain stimuli, including passive behaviours such as shyness or avoidance. The temperament we should strive for is 'neutral'. A neutral outlook is self-confident, respectful, interacts well and happy.

If you are unsure of your dog's temperament, seek professional advice, such as a dog behaviourist. They will be able to conduct some form of temperament testing and provide you with a report.

The behaviourist should also be able to identify if there are triggers to her temperament. It may be pain-related and therefore refer you to a vet for treatment, or they may identify specific dog training needs or, in fact, that they do not have a neutral temperament.

Though it takes two to tango in creating puppies because the females carry the puppies, they have more than 50% of the overall influence on them; it's believed to be as high as 80%.

In 2013, researchers at the University of Edinburgh led a study investigating the link between stress hormones and stress-related behaviour of newborn animals. They found that Cortisol (stress hormone) can cause the mother's placenta to shrink, directly affecting the fetus's developing brain due to the reduced flow of nutrients.

The researchers proved that increased exposure to Cortisol resulted in smaller pups, and these animals exhibited the signs of mood disorders (temperament issues). The research also showed how stress or trauma might negatively impact the genetic character of a pregnant female's unborn pups. The concept supports that stress can impact a female's fertility, pregnancy, and the unborn puppies she's carrying, affecting them later in life.

This highlights how vital it is for you to have identified your bitch's triggers and manage them to reduce the signs of stress if she is to be used in your breeding program. You'll also need to focus on any triggers as part of your puppy socialisation to prevent long-term generational problems for the pups in the litter. Following a program such as Puppy Culture or Avidog can be beneficial as they offer a comprehensive socialisation schedule for breeders to follow.

In the next chapter, let's look at the reality of dog breeding, reviewing some of my best and worst litters and why that may be the case.

Chapter 3 - Breeding Health summary

During this chapter, we have covered:

- The requirements of what is considered good canine health or breeding.
- The available dog health screening and its importance in improving the quality of puppies bred.
- How a dog's physical conformation may impact its health and the measures that can be taken to reduce associated risks.
- The importance of a neutral temperament and how you can actively select to breed for improvement.

CHAPTER 4

The Reality of Breeding

Dog breeding can look pretty glamorous; it doesn't take many scrolls on any social media platform to see reels of cute puppy bundles, perfectly posed pups and exciting breeding announcements.

On the surface, it all looks pretty straightforward and enticing, everything looks clean and tidy, but that is not the reality.

I'll see social stories of beautiful pups looking pretty perfect, whilst I have the same breeder on the phone near to tears because they are worried about them. They are unsure if the litter is fading or isn't growing well, weaning isn't going right, or mum refuses to feed them. One of the pups has a swollen eye, a funny squint, it's half the size or limping. The list of concerns is endless, but you won't see that posted on their feed or page.

It's all smoke and mirrors. If you do it with passion, breeding is hard work, tiring and stressful. If you are expecting the picture-perfect litter that you see others having, you need to re-think… you don't see the 3am puppy feeds, the fact they are too tired to get dressed, let alone clean the house. When they did leave the house, they were in a daydream bubble because they were so tired. How they feel agoraphobic due to not leaving the house for nearly three weeks or not realising they have puppy poo smeared down their top. The worry of making sure they are all placed in good homes, that they all pass their health checks or if the new owners will be pleasantly surprised with their new pooch.

It never stops; you'll just move from one worry to the next. It tends to be one hell of a bumpy ride that you won't be able to get off halfway through.

With my English Bulldogs litters, I often tell myself that I must be passionate about them because otherwise, I would be pretty darn stupid to keep signing up for this stress. I would have fewer grey hairs and more money in my pocket if I didn't breed them.

Breeding Expenses

As the owner of the female, it's your responsibility to plan and budget for your upcoming litter. Breeding isn't free, and rearing puppies all costs money. You will receive money for any puppies you subsequently sell, but it can take four months to generate these funds.

With that in mind, you should budget accordingly. I'm not going to make this chapter into a financial advice handbook, but be ready to budget for the following:

- Health testing
- Ovulation testing
- Travel to stud
- Stud fee
- Pregnancy detection
- Whelping equipment
- C-section & breeding related vet bills
- Puppy rearing costs - worming, weaning food, registration
- Puppy microchipping
- Puppy vet check & vaccinations
- Your time

Let's break these points down in more detail.

Health Testing

You should never breed two dogs with the same faults, and how do you know what these possible issues are unless you investigate and research? I covered in a previous chapter some of the health testing you should be considering for your female and equally looking for a stud to complement any requirements you may have. Do you need to lower a hip sore? Or require him to be DNA clear on a particular condition?

Health testing costs money, but that shouldn't be an excuse not to do it.

Hip and Elbow X-rays are one of the most expensive, costing from £350 to £500 depending on your location and the professional used.

DNA testing is around £60 a test, or you can choose to purchase a 'panel'. The panel is usually a group of tests between £150 to £300, but will include multiple tests, including coat colour and heritage, making them better value.

You'll also have your individual assessments for eyes, heart, hearing etc., and I would expect to pay around £100 per consultation.

It can all start to add up quickly, but many tests are once in a lifetime and will not change; others may need regular assessments, such as eyes.

Breeder Selling Skill Set

It's been said 'Everyone has become a marketer', and I believe it is true.

The role of a marketer is to get someone's attention, help them realise their problem and offer them a solution to fix the issue. You would have marketed yourself to your employer to obtain your job during an interview. They have a problem of a vacant position; your skillset is the solution. Even once you have the job, you market your skills to keep it. You market yourself to your clients when self-employed; you even market yourself to your partner to start a relationship and commit to it long term with marriage. We are selling ourselves all the time, whether we like it or not, and some are better at it than others.

Breeding dogs is no different; you'll need to market the puppies you've bred. What's your angle? Are the parent's health tested? Outstanding Bloodlines? Good Breed type? Holds accolades from canine activities such as exhibiting, working or agility? Puppy owners don't want to spend money on future heartache. They don't want to unknowingly buy a pup that's constantly at the vets or needs lifelong meds. They want to buy a bundle of joy that can bring them and their family many years of fun, and health testing is the only way they can make that vision a reality.

Health can't be guaranteed, but health testing will make you stand out from the crowd of other breeders. Health testing will reduce the risk of health issues as much as possible to avoid the headache of an unsatisfied puppy owner in 2, 4 or 6 months after the pup was sold.

Kennel Name

Another way to highlight your dogs as part of your marketing is to establish your breeding line by using a kennel name that can be seen and easily identified in future pedigrees (You'll find examples on the testimonial page). Kennel names are typically registered and recognised by Puppy Registering bodies and may also be referred to as an Affix. Due to so many different registries, some breeder's also choose to register their kennel name as a trademark with Intellectual Property Office (IPO), adding the additional protection of copyright laws. These require initial setup and renewal fees.

Ovulation Testing

Deciding not to have an ovulation test or use inferior methods can be counterproductive. You may feel like you are saving financially by not ovulation testing, but this approach lacks overall value. You will quickly diminish any savings you have made due to the additional matings and subsequent travel required to help increase the likelihood of pregnancy that wouldn't be needed if ovulation testing had been carried out.

Not mating at the most fertile time could result in smaller litters or no pups, or even worse, in my opinion, a solo puppy. In 2018, I reviewed my client data of 1,100 animals (mainly dogs) that I had scanned - 72% were positive pregnancies. Even more surprising was a 6.4% chance of the pregnancy being a solo puppy and only a 2.3% chance of the litter being 10 pups or more. I'm more likely to scan for a solo puppy than a big litter, no surprise, as large/giant breeds are less popular. This means solo puppy litters are more common than people realise.

From my observation, most solo pups are due to mating at the wrong time, either too early or too late. When this is the case, I like to try and guess the sex of the puppy. If you breed too late, it's more likely to be a male, and if you breed too early more likely to be female. Either way, solo puppies can be expensive, as the birth is more likely to be by c-section (elective at best or emergency at worse).

Hand rearing the puppy is also more likely if the Dam's milk does not typically come in. Solo puppies tend to seek human entertainment and interaction because they have no siblings to play with, so you'll spend more time keeping them mentally stimulated too.

With that said, all this will cost way more than some accurate ovulation testing. With that in mind, spending approx. £300 probably doesn't seem too bad to give you the best possible chance not only of success but a good-sized litter too.

Travel to Stud

Travel costs, this all needs to be factored into your breeding budget. For most, the ideal stud never lives round the corner - especially once you've invested in health testing, you'll find it will significantly narrow your field of selection. You could end up travelling the length and breadth of the country for the 'right boy'.

You only need something crazy like a fuel supply shortage to send your plans into disarray! However, I've had a fair few clients break down on the way or on the way home. Make sure your car is in tip-top condition for the travel because it could soon turn into a nightmare, breaking down in the summer with a dog and no functioning air conditioning.

Stud Fee

Stud fees can vary depending on the stud owner, the popularity, breed and physical demand.

An old rule of thumb was that a stud fee was the cost of a puppy. This meant that sometimes the stud owner would have '1st or 2nd pick' of litter, either because they have a keen interest in the breeding combination, the bitch owner may not have the initial funds, or they would be able to resell the puppy at a higher price than the stud fee. This is considered a 'pup back' deal.

In recent times the cost of a stud fee isn't always equal to the price of a puppy. It may be more or less depending on the breed.

Some stud owners may offer alternatives such as an initial smaller 'handling fee', and then either once the female is confirmed in pup or when puppies are born, the stud fee is due. These terms should only be offered to trusted relationships and agreed upon in advance due to the potential for deception.

Some stud owners will require the entire fee paid in advance or before the mating. Others may offer 'lock ins' where you can effectively agree to the "reduced" stud fee in advance and leave a deposit to secure at a set price. These stud owners believe the price or demand will increase over time. Once the stud's offspring have been seen or particular health checks have been obtained.

Pregnancy Detection

I'm biased, but I believe that if you have mated a female, you must ultrasound scan her to determine if she is pregnant. You can scan from 28 days from the last breeding. Knowing this key information early in the pregnancy allows you to plan appropriately. Scanning will also give you an approximate idea of puppy numbers, enabling you to actively manage your puppy waitlist, if you have one.

You can have your girl scanned at the vets, but nowadays, there are specialist professionals, many mobile, that will scan your girl in your own home, enabling you to experience the news first hand and ask any relevant breeding questions. Typically budget around £50 for this, or maybe £100 if you decide on a progress scan later in the pregnancy to check puppy development, formation and size.

If negative, you can start considering your Plan B a little sooner and decide what you could do differently to increase your chances of success next time.

It will also rule out other health conditions like Pyometra (Pyo, a uterus infection), which can give similar signs to pregnancy such as being lethargic, swollen abdomen and vaginal discharge. However, Pyo is a life-threatening condition if left undiagnosed and untreated.

Whelping Equipment

There are all kinds of puppy rearing equipment on the market, from the sublime to the ridiculous. If you aren't planning to breed frequently, you might not want to splash out on the all singing and dancing plastic system. Once-use cardboard whelping bed, DIY beds or lined puppy pen will probably see you from newborn to 8 weeks old. Typically the fancier the equipment, the more labour saving, easier to clean and easier to store when not in use.

Some breeds will use puppy incubators as they don't leave the dam unattended with the puppies due to clumsiness. An incubator provides a safe, temperature-controlled area, but a plastic tub with a heat mat, 3/4 covered with a towel, will achieve the same.

Incubators do, however, come into their own with a poorly puppy, especially ones that can be connected to oxygen, but an incubator will never cure a puppy. The puppy will still need a diagnosis and response to treatment to have any chance of survival. An incubator and oxygen supplementation will help ease distress but on their own, are unlikely to heal a declining puppy.

You will quickly burn through a ton of puppy pads when toilet training from 4 weeks of age. Many breeders have turned to using washable mats, which are more environmentally friendly, and more cost-effective over the long term, or litter tray training.

Puppy Rearing Costs

From newborn to 4 weeks, pups won't have too much of a financial impact if puppies are in good health because the dam will have supplied most of their requirements of food and warmth. Once you start to wean puppies, it can feel like they will eat you out of your house and home, depending on the breed and the litter size.

Initially, the costs will only be the increased food for the dam and puppy wormer. However, a Great Dane puppy at 8 weeks old will be eating around 1kg of raw food a day, probably around £4.80. So a litter of 10 would cost £336 to feed in their final week before leaving for their new home if they leave on time. And that's just food.

Additional costs will be associated if you plan to breed a pedigree registered litter. You'll also need to ensure both parents are registered with the same registry to register the litter. The stud owner will need to provide their male's registration details for you to register the litter, they may withhold this until the stud fee has been paid or the puppies have been born. The new puppy owners will typically pay an additional fee to transfer their puppy to them. Most registries will state that the papers are not proof of ownership, and this is why sales contracts should accompany any puppy when sold.

Registration Rights

Not all puppies are sold with registration papers (such as the KC). It's generally believed doing so will typically increase the puppy sale price because the puppies' heritage is confirmed.

Most registries will give you a choice when registering each puppy to put limitations on their papers, 'endorsements' for the puppy may include that they may not be exported and exhibited aboard or for offspring not to be registered. This is similar to other registries that allow the breeder to select Pet or Breeding papers for the puppy.

Breeders may wish to apply this condition because the puppy may not be of suitable breeding merit or to keep their bloodline exclusive. Whatever you decide, this must also be detailed in the sales contract, so the new puppy owners are fully aware of the dog's capability and expectations. In some particular breeds, the breeders have been known to 'early neuter spay' as young as 8 weeks old to control their bloodline. This long term decision means puppy owners know 100% that the puppy cannot be bred.

The puppy sale contracts should state that fertility when an adult is not guaranteed. During a puppy vet check, you may wish for it to be noted on the records if male puppies have descended testicles or not to prevent any future discrepancies.

Puppy Microchipping

Since April 2016, breeders have had the legal obligation to microchip their puppies before leaving for their new homes. It's the owners' responsibility to ensure the puppy's contact details are kept current.

This is a relatively straightforward process where a grain of rice sized microchip is placed under the skin on the scruff of the neck. Puppies are typically chipped from 6 weeks of age, costing around £10 to £25 per puppy. Puppies can be chipped by a vet or any trained professional. Many tend to offer a mobile service and can save you the logistical nightmare of moving a large litter to the local, potentially germ-ridden vet practice and back.

Puppy vet check & Vaccinations

There is no requirement for you to sell puppies with any vaccinations, but I recommend having every puppy's health checked before leaving for a new home. This will help you make better-informed choices when placing a puppy that may have a diagnosed health condition. Some vets will still charge consultation fees for this (dependant on litter size), and then it may become more cost-efficient to pay for the vaccinations due to their fee structure.

Most vet practices now offer Puppy Packs that may be discounted for breeders. They include vet check, vaccination course, microchipping, worming, flea treatment, free pet insurance, discount vouchers, and other marketing materials. It's most certainly worth finding out what your local vet practice offers to decide what route you wish to take.

C-section Cost

There's no getting around it, c-sections are expensive. I would budget for around £1,000- £3,000, depending on location and hours of operation.

Some breeds are more prone to a c-section due to inertia (contractions stop). This is either during the first stage when they haven't progressed into typical labour to deliver the pups or secondary inertia where they become tired and don't successfully deliver all the puppies naturally.

Other reasons may include a dam's narrow pelvis restricting a puppy from passing through and becoming stuck. Ultrasound scanning early in pregnancy will help identify the number of puppies to be expected, helping to manage the whelping process more effectively. Scanning with gestational measures could help provide due dates, which are vital if the female was not ovulation tested.

Using this information, you'll need to plan how best to avoid a c-section, working around any weekends or bank holidays. One of the benefits of Progesterone ovulation testing is that you'll know exactly when the female is full term. Some owners prefer an elective c-section, as this removes the stress and worry of an out of hours delivery, enabling them to manage cost. It also generally increases puppy survival rate, reducing the puppy losses per litter if delivery becomes difficult.

Some vets will insist on first stage labour before c-section, and given that this can last up to 36 hours, it may be possible to negotiate around weekends and out-of-hours charges.

Obviously, we hope and wish that the most natural route is taken and that the female self whelps the litter with little assistance, at home with your support. But you must understand that financially you can have a significant outlay if the birth doesn't go as planned.

Case Study of Costs

Here's a little case study of two litters I had less than a year apart. Both English Bulldogs scanned with above-average size litters. I wrote about Patsy in my first book, Not Born Yesterday. It was her first pregnancy and had been perfect until day 53 of gestation, then it rapidly declined. It seemed she was suffering from a rare condition called Maternal Hydrops, and it was agreed that we have to emergency c-section at 57 days to save her life. This resulted in eight deceased pups and her being spayed.

Then I had Aimee, sired by the same male as Patsy and also her first litter. She had a stress-free pregnancy, she self-whelped one pup, but we decided to c-section for the remaining litter due to inertia. All pups were strong, but she did develop mastitis. Two pups needed a cherry eye (when the third eyelid becomes inflamed and protrudes, becoming visually noticeable, like a cherry in the corner of the eye) removals.

Table of Costs	
Patsy – 2018 *(carrying 8 pups)*	**Aimee – 2017** *(carrying 9 pups)*
Pre-breeding testing (inc. Travel): £250 Stud fee: £700 Medical bills: £2,815 Weaning costs: £0 Vet check & Chip costs: £0 Registration: £0 Total Expenses: £3,765 Puppy Sales: £0 **Total = - £3,765**	Pre-breeding testing (inc. Travel): £220 Stud fee: £600 Medical bills: £2,585 Weaning costs: £508 Vet check & Chip costs: £270 Registration: £169 Total Expenses: £4,352 Puppy Sales: £17,500 *(+2 puppies kept)* **Total = + £13,148**

Regardless of how well the litter goes, you will still need to put aside around £4,000 to £4,500 to cover all possible expenses. From what I've observed since Brexit and the Pandemic, veterinary prices have increased, so I imagine it's now currently around £4,300 to £4,800. Even if you are lucky and no c-section is needed, expect you'll still need to budget around £1,000 - £2,000.

These figures need serious consideration and may not be realistic in everyone's budget. I don't know any vet practices that are happy to offer payment plans.

Required Breeding Effort

How much time and effort are we talking about?

Now you are comfortable that you've considered all aspects of your girl's health, you need to also consider the impact of rearing a litter on you and your family.

Rearing puppies is intensive, though it typically ends when they reach eight weeks. Many breeders end up extending how long they have the puppies due to the new owner's previous appointments that can't be rescheduled, you haven't sold all the puppies, or the puppies have been slow in development, and you decided to run them on a little longer. You'll need to factor this into how much time you have available.

Many breeders may use their employer's annual leave for the first few weeks of a litter, but this will still require family, friends, or even paid help to tend to the puppies if they can't frequently get home. Organising this may feel stressful or negatively impact the dam and her puppies.

If you live alone, just the simple task of taking a puppy to the vet and leaving the litter unattended can become a challenging problem. So solutions should be thought about and plans in place before the breeding has even happened because you certainly can't change your mind after.

To give you further insight, a newborn puppy will require around 12 feeds a day, approximately every 2 hours for nearly 2 whole weeks. Even if you have a breed that 'free feeds' from mum, you'll still need to monitor the puppies to ensure they are all feeding equally and monitor if any have been squashed or become chilled in the whelping box. If you have a more intensive breed with scheduled feeds (because they are kept separate from a clumsy mum), you might even have to toilet them every feed too.

All this is assuming puppies are healthy and robust, but what if you have a poorly puppy, an entire litter, or even worse, the litter is orphaned. If you can't locate a willing surrogate mum, you'll need to hand-rear the litter. If the litter is large, you could be consistently feeding puppies to ensure all are fed regularly.

I don't want to be all doom and gloom because if breeding was 'that bad' no-one would do it, and they certainly wouldn't do it regularly, but enough people do. Are these people juggling jobs, family, other dogs and puppy enquiries? Yes many are, but if I asked, how many of them found it easy? I think the response would be dire.

You need to be realistic about your capability to rear a problematic or demanding litter. You can't return the puppies once born for 'easier' ones.

Litter Whelping Services

A more recent phenomenon is the possibility of hiring a professional whelper to rear your litter for you. They will typically take the female and her puppies and rear them until an agreed age; for many, this is once weaning has started.

This kind of agreement directly conflicts with why many people breed, but I understand that this may be the only option in some circumstances. Significant trust is needed for this type of relationship due to the accountability and liability with puppy deaths or illnesses and how this is managed in the contract.

Some whelpers, if not local, may wish to use their own vet practice, so there also needs to be detailed contracts on the priority of care and how the expenses are to be settled if any treatment is needed. Agreements like this tend to be okay if all goes smoothly. When untypical incidents occur, all parties can disagree on the best path forward, so I recommend any bitch owners proceed with caution with these types of arrangements.

Let's look at how you can suitability prepare for puppies by ensuring your female is in the best condition for pregnancy.

Chapter 4 - Breeding health summary

During this chapter, we have covered:

- The real costs associated with breeding, and budgeting for all eventualities.
- The importance of establishing a breeding reputation, and how marketing will impact the sale of your puppies.
- The time and effort to be allocated to safely rear puppies, and alternative options.

CHAPTER 5

Pre-mating Preparations

Every other Sunday, I like to meet up with a good friend Charlotte, her husband Paul and the kids. We go on 'big dog' walks rotating between the beach and the forest. It started when I had Venice, an XL American Bully that needed to 'decompress' on a nice long, boundary-free run. Over time the dogs have changed, and they aren't always big sized dogs anymore.

One Sunday, I left home with just a Labrador in the car. I got a few yards down the road and could hear the weirdest noise that seemed familiar but not obvious. I pulled over, and my 19" alloy wheel was as flat as a pancake. Great. I was already running a little late, which is typical for anyone that knows me, and this certainly wasn't going to help.

Nowadays most cars don't come with a spare wheel, and to be honest, I'm not sure I could change it on a 4x4, even though it's a small one. What I had done many, many moons ago was by a can of tyreweld. I knew if you used this stuff in the back of my head, you'd definitely have to buy a new tyre, not just fix it (if fixable). That's fine, I thought, as the car was recently serviced, and I was notified that the tyres were starting to run low anyway and would need replacing.

I used the tyreweld, which inflated it enough to be drivable on B roads. As per the instructions, I planned to drive it and then put a little extra air in to fully inflate the tyre. Can you believe that the air compressor was out of action at the closest fuel station, and I didn't want to stop driving, so I slowly coasted to meet up with Charlotte and Paul.

En route, I phoned the Kwikfit closest to our walk and explained I was driving to them to get a new tyre. The receptionist informed me they were pretty busy but would do their best to fit me in. I then phoned Charlotte and asked if it was okay that they meet me at Kwikfit and make room for the dog and me.

I'm not sure how they define busy on arrival, but one car was being worked on, and no one was in the waiting room.

I explained to the tyre fitter that I was off for a dog walk and that I'd be back in an hour or so, and if he could squeeze me in, I'd be super appreciative. I asked for the budget tyre to be put on, mainly because it was an unexpected expense, and the car was being sold at some point in the near future anyway.

After a few moments of him pulling numerous serious faces at his PC, he explained that he couldn't get a budget in stock until tomorrow and that he only had a Continental Sports Contact 5 in stock which was just shy of £250.

Wow, that's the most expensive dog walk I had ever been on.

I told him to crack on and fit the tyre, I had no choice. Tomorrow I had a full day of mobile work booked, and it wasn't worth the drama of attempting to reschedule everyone.

I try to take the positive out of most situations, and my first initial thought was, thankfully I found the puncture on a Sunday rather than on a Monday morning when I was heading out the door. I was also really pleased that I had the can of tyreweld, I have no recollection of when I bought it, but it had sat in my car for a long time.

Even when I was filling up the tyre, the owner of the house I stopped outside came out to check what had happened. I explained that I would use the tyreweld and carry on my day if possible. They remarked they would have just turned around and gone back home.

Well I didn't, the dog still got walked, I still met my friends and the car still got fixed (even if my purse was a lot lighter) and Monday's clients remained scheduled.

What was the first thing I did the following day? Bought another can of tyreweld, it didn't fix the issue, but it stopped my day spiralling out of control. It was a temporary fix that I could initiate until I sorted a long term solution.

So why am I telling you this?

Being prepared in life will get you far, in Not Born Yesterday, I talked about the 7 P's.

In a past life, when I was a Learning & Development Consultant working for various corporate companies, I used to train the '5P's of Planning' in management workshops.

1. Proper
2. Planning
3. Prevents
4. Poor
5. Performance

I prefer the 6 P's - Proper Planning Prevents Piss Poor Performance, to drive the point home. Either way, the model encourages you to consider and act on a situation, helping you avoid problems, drama and unnecessary emotional stress. Relevant for dog breeding, I created my own 7P's.

1. Proper
2. Planning
3. Prevents
4. Problem
5. Pregnancies &
6. Poorly
7. Pups

And I still stand by this.

Taking proactive behaviour in your decision making will help you prevent problems and potential disasters.

Being prepared will help you feel more in control. Though you might not have the resolution, you'll probably be able to muddle your way through, ultimately resulting in a successful, enjoyable outcome. So let's look at what can be done to suitably prepare yourself and your bitch.

Fertility Obstacles

You'll be surprised by the possible obstacles that may stop you from breeding your female when you intended. The following covers the primary considerations that need to be made before deciding to breed.

Breeding age

If you are breeding a pedigree dog, and puppies are to be registered with the Kennel Club, then the breeding female must be over 12 months old. There are some additional advisories for giant breeds, to push back until at least 20 months of age due to their slower development and maturity patterns.

It's deemed poor practice to breed any female on her first season regardless of what age it occurs, even if she is over 12 months of age. I personally prefer to breed from the absolute earliest of 18 months of age, or from her third season.

You must check the minimum breeding age if you breed a dog under an alternative registration system, such as ABKC, EBKC, UKC or DWKC. These time frames help the female mature physically and mentally, giving time for any issues with her own health to become apparent before breeding.

Different breeds mature at different rates. Large and giant breeds tend to be significantly slower. Young minded females are more likely to struggle with the concept of pregnancy and rearing puppies, which could result in confusion, poor puppy acceptance, cannibalism and ultimately, you have to hand-rear the puppies. Mental maturity and stability of temperament must be considered before breeding, regardless of age.

The Kennel Club also requires special permission for females to be bred over eight years, meaning you have a seven-year breeding window, around 10 to 12 seasons. It's widely accepted that it's favourable for a female to have her first litter before four years. It's also believed breeding an older bitch for the first time can lead to more problematic pregnancy and birth. No different to humans, where pregnancy over 35 years old is classed as a geriatric and is associated with more complications, including an increased chance of miscarriage and birth defects.

Breeding Restrictions

You must also check if you have 'breeding rights' on your female. If she is listed on a breed register, you must check that the registration gives you the right to register any resulting offspring.

Some dog registrations may have 'endorsed' pedigrees where the breeder has stipulated that the female should not be bred. This may be due to a health condition or simply to control their bloodline. Any conditions of this nature should have been documented in the sales contracts on purchase; this may also have been identified when provided with 'Breeding' or 'Pet' registration papers.

Even if the female is not registered, it's beneficial to have full awareness of her reproductive status. Particularly if you acquired her as an adult. Has she had any previous litters? If so, how many and how did the pregnancy and delivery go?

Conditions such as ovarian remnant syndrome (ORS) can give the impression that the female is in season when she cannot conceive.

Fertility History

Many people have informed me how they rescued a dog and decided to breed from them. I realised that they weren't 'rescued' per se, most rescue centres and shelters will neuter dogs before being placed in their new homes. They often meant that they hadn't pro-actively looked for a breeder, picked a puppy intending to breed, and come home with it. They seem to have acquired a dog through friends or family or been given an opportunity to own a dog for one reason or another and taken it.

When you haven't had a dog 'from new' (a puppy) it's essential to find out if she has had previous litters, how she was as a mum and whether she has been spayed. It's not as easy as saying well she has seasons, so she must be entire. The Royal College of Veterinary Science (RVCS) suggest that females can be spayed from 4 months old. Although, most Breeders are more likely to suggest from 18 months once the dog has become an adult and finished many vital hormonal stages.

Some breeds and breeders will juvenile (early neuter) spay as young as 8 weeks old before the puppy leaves for its new home. It's not just as clear cut as buying a puppy and assuming it will be intact, and these discussions should be had in advance of the purchase or collection.

Ovarian Remnant Syndrome (ORS)

Ovarian Remnant Syndrome (ORS) can occur in 17% of spays. The condition occurs when ovarian tissue wrongly remains inside the body once a female has been spayed. Ovariectomy (OVE), where the just ovaries are removed, or ovariohysterectomy (OVH), the ovaries and uterus are removed. The remaining tissue can produce oestrogen, triggering signs of a season. This is not only misleading but confusing. Every season, you could breed this female, but she would never conceive because it's not physically possible.

It's vital to know your girl's previous breeding history, if any, and fertility status.

It's also worth considering the long term impact it will have on the female. We've already covered the do's and dont's when it comes to the age range, but also consider the toll it will take on a female rearing up to four large litters. I've pretty much bred from every dog I've owned, when it's been feasible, apart from my French Bulldog, Hunni (nicknamed potato on legs by the Rose family).

She was the third generation of French Bulldogs I had bred, but I decided I wanted to focus on my primary breed, English Bulldogs, as I was doing so well with them. So the French Bulldogs went on the back burner. Before we knew it, she was a veteran (over 7 years old), plus we had no desire to breed from her.

Hunni's Grand dam declined quickly in health just after, passing her 7th birthday with no accurate diagnosis. Her daughter (Hunni's mum) made it to 9 years of age, outliving her Dam but passing with very similar symptoms. Hunni and her siblings are now 10.5 years old and still going strong as I type this. It might just be a coincidence, and I'll never fully know (as I'm sure all the dogs I'll have going forward will be pro-actively part of my breeding program), to me, the fact that she hasn't had a litter has most certainly added years to her existence, and I do genuinely believe that breeding can impact a dog's longevity.

Even if not directly, indirectly over time. As they age, the evidence shows litters may impact cell renewal, healing and general recovery opportunities.

The Female Heat

Identifying day one of your female's season when you plan to breed is important; it has many associated triggers and actions. Firstly we need to understand a little about a female heat or season. The heat is, in fact, a fertility cycle that can be split into 4 sections, each then feeding into the other in a loop. Understanding these phases will help you ensure success with a litter. Let's look at each phase and what that means regarding you managing her season.

- **Proestrus** is a phase lasting approximately 8-10 days. The female is considered in heat, and you'll see physical changes such as her vulva swelling and bloody discharge. You may also witness temperament changes, she may be more lethargic or moody.

- **Oestrus** lasts around 8-10 days and is considered the ovulation and fertile phase. The discharge often becomes pinkish red or may even stop. The female becomes receptive to males at this time; depending on the female, she may attempt to gain attention by backing up to males, lifting or flagging her tail to one side.

When touched around her back legs, she may also be sensitive, lifting her vulva in response. During this phase, the eggs have been released and will be ready for fertilising by sperm that successfully make it through the cervix.

- **Diestrus** is the phase that can last just over eight weeks and is the non-fertile window ending the heat. Bloody discharge can still occur, and any females may still be willing to mate, but the eggs released for conception are ageing and become no longer viable.

- **Anoestrus** is the part of the cycle that is the longest, typically lasting 5-9 months. There is no bleeding, the female is not fertile, and it is considered a dormant phase.

The timescales of each phase are averages, and that's the problem. If your female's body followed the above, then breeding would be much easier, but that certainly isn't what is experienced by many.

The cycle can also be different for each female and depending on her breed. Most breeds will cycle every six to nine months, some going as long as 12 months, particularly in their first season.

Add the complexity of owning more than one female or having a clean and tidy dog. Females will generally season together, making it even more challenging to identify who is in which phase of their heat.

As an owner, we need to identify the oestrus phase of the cycle. This is when she will be ovulating and deemed in her most fertile window for conception. For this reason, many owners do ovulation test to help pinpoint the most optimal time to breed, which we will look at a little further in this book.

Silent Seasons

Ovulation testing will help females who have blind or silent seasons. These females show minimal physical or behavioural changes and lack discharge, to the point it amazes me how observant some owners are to know they are even possibly in season. Progesterone ovulation blood testing can help identify these types of seasons.

Silent/dry seasons may be caused by underlying undiagnosed medical conditions, particularly if the female fails to conceive when bred. These would typically be hormone-related, and it would be worth investigating conditions such as Addison Disease (lower hormone output of the adrenal gland), Cushing's Disease (endocrine syndrome due to pituitary or adrenal gland) or an under-active Thyroid gland.

Split Seasons

Progesterone ovulation testing will also identify split or non-ovulating seasons, which helps build a picture of that particular female's ovulation pattern. Typically once the Progesterone levels start to rise, they should continue. Some females can plateau and sit at the same level for a few days before an increase, or they can even then decline, which confirms the female is having a non-ovulating or split season.

A split season is when a female will have a 'typical' season but never actually ovulate and then come back into season after a short period. During the second part of the heat, they ovulate and can conceive.

This could mean you've wasted a lot of time, energy and effort if you covered the female in the first half of the season, as you didn't test, and you'll need to repeat the process next time in the latter half.

Progesterone ovulation testing will also help rule out life-threatening conditions, such as Pyometra (uterus infection), that a breeder could easily mistake as the female being in season. On all accounts, testing will save you time and money on non-productive and pointless matings.

Back-to-Back Breeding

The Kennel Club would register a maximum of four litters to one female and only two if the litters were born by c-section.

They also recommend a female should not whelp two litters within 12 months. The dog breeding licence also backs this ethos. These conditions are to safeguard the female and her health. However back-to-back breeding, which is two consecutive litters with no 'rest' season, does not breach the Kennel Club's B22 Regulation, so they will register pups born.

In recent years and with the support of the internet, there has been a considerable debate over the ethics and impacts of 'back to back' breeding.

The opinion that seems to be U.S research-led is that back-to-back breeding is more beneficial for the female. I don't believe there is a right or wrong with debates like this, but most certainly lots of opinions. Also, consider how cognitive dissonance may or may not impact your thoughts and choices on such an emotive topic.

The argument is that she'll have her litters whilst younger, typically her first litter, followed quickly by her second. A heat missed, and she's then mated on the next for her third litter, followed by a fourth (should it be suitable) and then be neutered, or possibly three consecutively, then spayed.

The counter-argument often used is that back-to-back breedings help reduce the likelihood of Pyometra (a uterus infection). While a female cannot develop Pyometra if pregnant, infection rates are extremely low in young females, so this point alone is not a reason to back-to-back.

Breeding from a 'younger and healthier' uterus with fewer heats, and therefore fewer effects of progesterone (which can trigger related health conditions), is believed to be beneficial, but a female should not just be classified by her uterus.

Firstly, just because I said four litters, not all bitches need or should have four. The health of the bitch and how she coped with her previous litters should be considered every time before breeding. Remember:

"Ethical behaviour is doing the right thing when no one else is watching — even when doing the wrong thing is legal."

Aldo Leopold

You must also consider the breed 'norms'; some breeds slow development means they would typically only have three litters and possibly even less if they are by c-section.

The counter-argument is that a bitch should be given sufficient time to recover, so breeding on the next heat could be more damaging. You'll need to acknowledge her previous litter size, how they were delivered and if there were any other complications. If a female were to cycle every 12 months, the back-to-back breeding method might not cause any issues.

Given the typical time frame is 6 months, it should be given serious thought for its suitability. I have known breeders back-to-back with small litters or solo pups that have taken minimal effort for the dam to raise, meaning no condition was lost.

Breeding so frequently also raises additional questions, such as ensuring you have future puppy owners for this continual quantity of puppies. The feedback on puppy quality is also difficult to gauge when you restrict the time between litters. As a breeder, you'll be unsure if that particular breeding combination was 'the best', as the puppies haven't yet grown and matured to adulthood to see the final effect. You could repeat a breeding, and should some health issues come to light in the future, you will have doubled the potential number of impacted puppies from repeating the breeding so quickly. Seeing the quality of a breeding program takes years to develop and observe.

It's worth noting that some bitches will continue to cycle as if they've never had a litter. In contrast, others will 'reset' their cycle from the birth of the pups, meaning the period between a litter and the following season may be extended but then will continue with regular frequency as they previously did.

If you are still contemplating it, check with your registry if back-to-back breeding is acceptable in their breeding code of ethics.

When to Spay?

I need to cover spaying to provide the complete picture of breeding. Another reason 'back to back' seems to be becoming more popular is it allows some breeders to rehome or place the female into a pet home whilst younger due to whelping and rearing her litters sooner.

Some deem this a 'commercial' approach to breeding that has (in my opinion) only been encouraged by the Breeding Licence restrictions placed on the number of dogs that can be in a household with the criteria asking what the 'exit plan' is for ex-brood bitches.

This is a reason that, personally, I prefer co-owning dogs. The female can live in their forever home from a puppy, on the condition she is returned for breeding when of suitable age and subject to health tests. Co-ownership comes with its own complexities and requires strong commitment and trust, so much so that some breeders prefer not to take this option at all.

Pyometra

Another hot topic is whether to spay when a female has her final c-section. Spaying a female is favourable for stopping further seasons, but it also diminishes the threat of Pyometra (pyo), a deadly uterus infection.

There's a 1 in 4 chance of a female developing the condition when they have reached the age of 10. The risk increases with age, but younger individuals can also be affected occasionally. Hormonal treatments given to prevent seasons or after an accidental mating to prevent pregnancy are thought to increase the risk of pyo.

The death rate is around 5% with treatment, and without, death should be considered a certainty. Symptoms develop typically 2 months after a season and can be easily confused with pregnancy; these include lethargy, vomiting, diarrhoea, increased thirst, enlarged abdomen and lack of appetite.

The only way to prevent Pyo in an entire bitch is to ensure she's pregnant. This fact supports 'back to back' breeding. Although note, as I said earlier, the risk in younger bitches is lower.

Some breeders may choose to spay during a c-section, saving on additional anaesthetic, vet bills and unknown risks with a separate operation. This is only really an option for breeders who decide to elective c-section, as an emergency is probably due to an imperative health risk that takes priority unless a spay is recommended as part of the treatment.

The concern is could spaying negatively impact milk production, and with this in mind, many breeders decide not to spay. Rearing a litter when the dam has no milk (Agalactia) will be significantly more challenging, as you'll need to hand-rear the puppies by supplement feeding.

There are a few things to consider. The first is that milk production is generated from the Pituitary gland that sits near the brain (not the ovaries that are to be removed for spaying), so milk production should not technically be impacted.

The second is how well the female has produced milk in her previous litters, which may also be breed dependent. From my experience, French Bulldogs have milk spurting out of every hole soon after pups are born. English Bulldogs are notoriously slow in producing milk, meaning most puppies will lose weight for 3-4 days before they start to gain. I would not hesitate to section-spay a French Bulldog with this breed knowledge but certainly would an English Bulldog.

I believe that c-sectioning too early would negatively impact milk production more than spaying during the c-section. Sectioning too early could lead to a lack of Oxytocin (the hormone produced in the Pituitary gland released during labour and whelping).

Before you decide, consider each bitch on their own merit and ask for your vet's advice and opinion.

As a side note, you have two options for spaying your female. The first is an open spay, this is the traditional method. If done during a c-section, this is the type of spay your female will have using the incision made to remove the pups and remove the uterus and ovaries (ovariohysterectomy). The concern is that you are removing reproductive organs at their most sensitive and heightened state.

Laparoscopic spays are becoming a popular alternative choice for owners. This is a keyhole spay where just the ovaries are removed (Ovariectomy). Due to the nature of the procedure, there is less pain and faster recovery.

The operational time for the keyhole procedure is around 45 minutes, compared to an open spay of around 20 minutes and typically is around £180 more expensive due to the specialised equipment used. Not all vet practices can offer a laparoscopic spay, as they do not have the equipment, whilst also factoring in the additional theatre time and skill required.

If you decide to spay at a later stage, this would typically be 3 months after a litter or during the Diestrus (dormant) phase of a season. Though some vets may say it's possible to carry out sooner.

Milk Myth

It is a myth that feeding milk, normally goats or puppy formula to the mum helps her produce more milk. She just needs high-quality food and plenty of fresh water.

78% of the milk she produces is water. Most females will have a 3-4 day water reserve post-whelp for milk production, so don't be too concerned if she doesn't consume much fluid initially.

You will know when her milk is developing, as she will pant and shake, particularly when feeding the puppies, but she should not have a high temperature.

Feeding her milk will just help with her overall body condition because it's a relatively easy way to consume a high number of calories.

Induced seasons

We've covered bitches with regular cycles, but some females don't run like clockwork, resulting in irregular seasons. Inducing a season is not a routine procedure but is worth being aware of. Only your vet should prescribe any treatments after a comprehensive discussion, including any potential risks.

It may be something you would need to consider if you had an ageing female who had failed to conceive on previous breedings, and the time between her cycles is elongated, or females whose frequency of heats varies wildly.

Galastop, which is also used for phantom/false pregnancies symptoms, can be used. Typically 80% of bitches will respond, but the treatment can be quite costly due to calculation by weight. Once pro-oestrus has started, the season will be normal with typical fertility. From my limited knowledge in this area, these treatments cannot be administered to a female who has never had a noticeable season.

Products like Receptal and PG600 are formulated for cattle and will induce ovulation, improve conception rates and help the farmer synchronise ovulation, helping them manage their breeding schedules.

These are not canine products and should not be used as such. I've heard and seen various channels advertising and offering questionable services. You don't have to Google too hard to find the 'Veterinary Medicines Directorate' investigation with Defra Investigation Services and the local police raiding and seizing such non-UK veterinary products and Prescription only medicine from unregulated canine fertility clinics.

If you have such issues, research your nearest qualified canine reproduction veterinary professional, or ask your local vet for a referral.

Chapter 5 - Pre-mating Preparations summary

During this chapter, we have covered:

- That correctly planning and preparing when breeding is vital for pregnancy success.
- All the phases of a female canine fertility cycle, and why ovulation testing is beneficial.
- Health issues and conditions that may negatively impact fertility and conception.

CHAPTER 6

Pregnancy Supplements

There are not many things you need to do before she's in season. She should be in good health and body condition before breeding. Free of any illness or detrimental hereditary conditions, with a good appetite and suitable quality food.

You have complete control over the health of your female before breeding, which can directly impact how well she copes with the breeding experience and any subsequent surgery.

Vitamins and minerals are essential to help a body function and repair. Supplements may need to be given to boost the body's system should the diet not provide the complete requirements or if the growth stage of the dog alters. Supplementation should be started before the season, at least 3 months before, to be fully metabolised into the body's system.

Vitamin E - wheat germ oil

Supplements such as wheat germ oil, a natural source of vitamin E, are an antioxidant for the reproductive organs. This aids fertility by removing harmful free radicals formed as a by-product of everyday metabolism as the body converts food and water into energy. It's also suitable for females with inconsistent seasons to help stabilise and regulate them.

Free radicals can damage cells. It is invaluable to ensure a plentiful supply of vitamin E to scavenge and protect against these.

Vitamin E is also essential for the healthy function of skin, coat and the nervous system; it's widely used to help maintain fertility and a healthy reproductive system in male and female dogs.

Folic Acid

I recommend Folic Acid for the flat-faced (brachycephalic) breeds because the formation of their muzzle is different due to the shortened length.

Royal Canin supported a study that confirmed that folate supplementation during a bitch's pregnancy could significantly reduce the risks of cleft palate by nearly 50%.

Some foods will have an elevated folate level, but generally, it's not enough for the brachy breeds. It's recommended to give 5mg per day. Optimal supplementation is 15 days before mating until puppies are born.

Medical Treatments

My preference is to keep medical treatments to a minimum when your female is in season and throughout the pregnancy.

Ticks

Ticks are spider-like tiny parasites that suck the blood from other animals. They have 8 legs with an egg-shaped body that will become larger and darker when filled with blood. Most vets recommend spot-on treatments or tablets; my preference would be to avoid these, and if one is discovered, use a 'tick tool' to remove them promptly.

Flea Treatments

I'm not a fan of flea treatments once in season, especially if no fleas are even present. If in doubt, seek veterinary advice for suitability. There are a few 'safe' flea treatments for pregnant dogs, including Frontline (Fipronil based) and Advocate (Imidacloprid and Moxidectin based). A flea comb is an excellent method to remove adult fleas, but it won't break the cycle if eggs have already been deposited around the home, so a topical household treatment may be required.

Worming

The majority of vets will suggest that you worm your dog at around 40 days gestation and again when the pups are 2 weeks old to prevent the transfer and cycle of worms.

They usually recommend Panacur, as its active ingredient, Fenbendazole, is deemed safe during pregnancy. It typically does not cover Lungworm. Drop-on Advocate if given monthly, will treat lungworm, but there have been no safety studies on the suitability during pregnancy and lactation.

I had an insightful conversation with the Laboratory Director and Senior Analyst at wormcount.com, Michaela Murray at Crufts 2018. Michaela explained the issue with worms possibly becoming resistant to chemical wormers and problems that may arise if we continue to overuse and treat dogs indiscriminately.

Instead of fretting about which wormers are needed and when you could test your girl's stool to see if she has worms at 40 days gestation. Should the result be positive, you will be advised to specifically treat the type of worm she has, rather than blindly treating all.

Michaela recommends collectively testing the puppies when they are 2 weeks old. If positive, you treat the puppies and mum. If negative, then no treatment is required.

You then carry out one final collective check when the puppies are 7 weeks old, for which certificates can be provided for your puppy packs detailing the puppy's worm status. This is a super way to ensure you're not putting too many chemicals into mum or the puppies and is a lot more effective method to target and treat any specific issues they may have.

You can order the testing kits directly through Wormcount's website - it's a postal service, and you'll be provided with a kit to return a small sample of faeces by Royal Mail.

Vaccinations

Puppies inherit a great deal of health and immunity from their mother immediately following birth from the colostrum (first form of milk) for up to 12 hours.

For this reason, your girl should be up-to-date with her annual boosters. But even if they have lapsed by a year or so, it's generally acceptable to delay vaccinations until after the puppies are born because the dam will still have a level of protection.

Dogs that have never been vaccinated should consider deactivated vaccines (non-live) alternatives, which are more expensive than standard vaccines. But they may also have some other limitations, including delaying the puppies' own vaccination.

Vaccicheck

If you want to know your girl's existing immunity levels - without indiscriminately vaccinating or are unsure of the dog's current vaccination status. You have the option of an Antibody Titer test. This test requires a small amount of blood/serum to ascertain current levels against Infectious Hepatitis (ICH), Parvovirus (CPV) & Distemper (CDV).

Not all vets offer this alternative service, so you will need to research your nearest participating practice.

Antibiotics

Vaginitis is inflammation of the vagina, usually caused by bacterial infection. Vaginitis can be triggered for many reasons, including trauma, urinary and uterus infections, herpes virus and vaginal anatomical defects (strictures). Poor vaginal drainage due to strictures during a season can also trigger vaginitis.

If your bitch has previously missed, you may want to consider putting her on a short course of broad-spectrum antibiotics when in season in case of the condition. Most vets will advise against this protocol as a preventative measure, but they should be willing if provided with the historical information of having not conceived on previous breedings. Frequent use of antibiotics can cause yeast infections, so they shouldn't be used carelessly; there are also concerns about antibiotic resistance.

Canine Herpes Vaccine (CHV)

Herpes Caninum is transmitted through any dog-to-dog contact. It's challenging to test for, and it's believed to cause neonatal puppy losses, foetal absorptions and abortions. I have the school of thought, "if it's not broken, don't fix it", so I wouldn't routinely consider this vaccination unless I personally had a female with pregnancy issues or puppy losses. I would then consider it for any future breedings.

The vaccine can be hard to source as there are frequent supply issues and rumours that the manufacture of the product may soon be stopped, so have the conversation with your vet well in advance of requiring it.

It's typically given by injection two weeks after mating and again two weeks before puppies are due, helping to boost the dam's immune system in favour of the puppies she is carrying. I have heard of alternative homoeopathic remedies but they may be worth researching, but they are unsure of their effectiveness.

Dam's Diet

Initially you don't need to make any changes to her diet if it's good quality. Only once pregnancy is confirmed will you need to act. It's always good to consider what options you have in advance.

Many working kennels make minimal changes to the food type or quantity until puppies are born; the same applies to small confirmed litters or solo pups. Minimal increases in food avoid encouraging puppies to grow large and the associated potential issues of getting stuck during birth from being over-sized. However, even an average-sized puppy can still become stuck due to a dam's narrow pelvis - and you won't know your dam's pelvis size and possible issues until she attempts to labour and delivers the pups.

If you decide to increase food amounts during pregnancy, it should be no more than 10% a week from the fifth week of gestation. A high-quality food can be given from the seventh week (many such products contain 22% Protein levels, 8% Fat, 1% Calcium and 0.8% Phosphorus).

Most breeders transfer the dam onto the same food brand but the Puppy variety in the final two weeks. Offering a higher nutritional quality in the same quantity of food, alleviating any uncomfortable full tummies, particularly when carrying large litters.

Some breeders will transfer to wet or raw food (if previously fed kibble) for the final weeks. This is believed to reduce the likelihood of 'water puppies', which some associate with high sodium diets. These puppies retain water and are oversized or jellified. Research has been conducted, and it's also believed the compatibility of the parents' blood types may also be accountable.

The breeds predisposed to these issues include (but are not limited to) Bulldogs, English Mastiffs, French Bulldogs, Pugs and Boston Terriers. A wet or raw meal is also more comfortable for the dam, due to less bloating after the food is eaten. Equally, kibble food can be soaked in water before feeding, so bloating is less likely.

A female will gain around 25-30% of her weight due to her pregnancy by 9 weeks gestation. She must be in the best body condition before breeding.

1 lb of sugar is nearly half a kilo, this means an English Bulldog around 28kg, would gain 4.4kg, which is 9 bags of sugar, but a Great Dane at 60kg would gain 18kg (which is the equivalent of a Cavalier King Charles Spaniel in weight!).

Once puppies are born, allowing the Dam to free feed (by leaving an unlimited amount of food in the bowl so she can graze) will help produce quality milk for the pups to thrive until weaning. Raw red meats such as lamb and beef can help with a dam's milk production. People also like to feed a Fenugreek supplement to encourage milk.

If you raw feed, the amount of Bone (Calcium) should be reduced in her diet from 6 weeks gestation; this will help soften bowel movements, making her more comfortable. Stool observation is also a good way of understanding your female's Calcium level requirements which can be connected to conditions such as Eclampsia, which can be fatal. It's widely accepted that edible bone should be reduced from 6 weeks gestation and then increased once pups are born, but I recommend you seek advice from your food manufacturer directly for the best approach.

Talking of food, let's see how I got in a hot mess with milk at the airport and what's that got to do with ovulation detection.

Chapter 6 - Pregnancy Supplements summary

During this chapter, we have covered:

- The benefits dietary supplements can bring during pregnancy.
- Which medications and treatments may be required whilst pregnant and their potential impact.
- How a dam's dietary requirements will change during pregnancy.

CHAPTER 7

Ovulation Detection

As a child, I was fortunate to holiday a lot. Raised in a single-parent family, my mother always managed to get the funds for my brothers and me to go abroad for the summer. Greece, Crete, Spain, Egypt and Florida, to name a few. Often in self-catering accommodation, my mother always felt the need to smuggle some English provisions.

Namely Tetley tea bags and milk, a true Brit - you can't beat a good brew. I remember her asking for me to put a litre carton of UHT semi-skimmed milk in my hand luggage on one holiday. I will show my age because this was way before the airport fluid limits and restrictions you commonly experience today.

No questions asked. I shoved it in my bag and probably moaned about how heavy it was at every opportunity.

All was fine until it came to airport security.

I put my bag on the conveyor belt and walked through the scanner with no problems. We would holiday with one or two other families in those days, so it was slight carnage with kids and the odd parent trying to round us up like sheep.

I was asked by the security, who, given my age, looked massively scary and intimidating, if the bag was mine. I fessed up that it was, and he asked me to step to one side and explain what was in it.

Like a scene from the Generation Game, I tried to recall, felt tip pens? A crossword and puzzle book? Maybe some hair scrunchies? I dunno. What else does a kid pack? Whilst feeling the creeping emotion of wanting to just burst into tears.

My mother realised a situation was developing and was by my side to find out what was happening.

It transpired the carton of milk she gave me showed up as a solid black mass on the scanning machine. It could have been anything, and we all know of the horrors that have unfolded on scheduled flights since.

Thanks, Mum. With family like that, who needs enemies.

As a breeder, you need to be the security guard for your dogs and be vigilant with your observations. Making an effort to detect when your female is ovulating is critical. Knowing what's going on the 'inside' of your bitch will make your breeding journey easier, helping you get to your chosen destination of 'Puppy Paradise' much sooner. You can't see inside your bitch, but you can look for the signs and use the available equipment and science.

The purpose of ovulation detection

As a breeder, it's vital to identify the oestrus phase of your girl's cycle. This is when she will be ovulating and deemed in her most fertile window for conception if mated.

Identifying this phase helps you know precisely when to mate. If you plan to travel a significant distance for your stud dog, this will help with the logistics.

It's also vital information for a stud handler to know. Forcing a natural mating when the bitch is not ready can be highly distressing to the female, impacting her willingness to mate on subsequent litters. It can also put the stud at risk of being attacked or injured during a mating and negatively impact his confidence with future breedings. The negative experience for both dogs (particularly during their second fear phase) could have a long-term detrimental impact.

The stud owner may handle their own dog, but it's also common for experienced handlers to be hired. Ovulation testing will also help you manage costs effectively, requiring fewer matings, saving time, effort and cost of travel.

Testing will also prevent a stud dog from being overused. Some stud owners insist on the female owner ovulation testing to protect their dog and ensure all bitches he serves are treated with the same merit and consideration.

Pinpointing when your female has ovulated ensures you breed at the most optimal time, resulting in bigger overall litter sizes.

A dog pregnancy is typically 63 days from ovulation, not from mating as many believe. So by knowing when she ovulated, you have a much more accurate due date. This is hugely advantageous for organising elective c-sections and helping to increase puppy survival rate. It also helps you manage your diary, organising any additional support or assistance needed for the expected delivery, particularly with weekends and bank holidays.

This additional information is like having another jigsaw puzzle piece and helps you build a picture of what's happening for each planned breeding. The more puzzle pieces, the more information, the less unexpected dramas - remember the 7P's to preparation.

There are many options available to detect when your female is ovulating. Although, Progesterone ovulation testing is the only method to be recognised as accurate by the medical and veterinary profession, we will consider the majority of products currently available on the market.

The female heat is a cycle, and the time in each phase can vary, female to female and season to season. We can assume that some bitches fertility is not fixed. Even if you have progesterone tested previously and confirmed she had ovulated on day 12 of her last season, there is no guarantee that the next season, she'll ovulate the same. Not to mention the possible human error of correctly identifying day 1 of the season. You can build up an ovulation pattern from previous testing, and will know if she's roughly an early, average or late ovulater. You can then use that insight to help you decide when to start testing for any subsequent breedings.

From my experience, I've seen girls switch between early to average or average to late, but I've never seen them jump from early to late or vice versa.

Methods of detecting ovulation

So what are the options?

There's a lot out there for you to pick from. However, the success rate and accuracy of many are questionable. Let's briefly run through some of the current popular options because, ultimately, getting this part right will significantly impact achieving your breeding goals, like the corner pieces of a jigsaw puzzle.

Methods have been categorised by cost to create some form of scale whilst measured against reliability, inferring the overall value. You can decide if investing a little more during the breedable season makes you a more successful breeder.

No Cost - Low Value Options

These methods might be favoured because they are 'free', and that's not a word you'll often hear when breeding. The effort required for these methods is limited, and accuracy is considered relatively unknown.

Experienced stud dog

You may be lucky to come across an experienced stud who is confident in mating various temperament bitches (both the willing and unwilling) and has the sixth sense to only mate when a bitch is ready. This means they have outstanding sensory skills to identify a female in the oestrus phase of her cycle from the pheromones she is releasing.

If the stud can mate and achieve a tie (where the two dogs lock together for some time), you would consider this a successful mating, but not necessarily successful breeding until the female is confirmed pregnant.

With this approach, many people experience a 'slip tie' when the dog has mounted and ejaculated inside the female, but there was no tie or lock. The handler may have to hold them together to prolong the mating to improve the success rate. Bitches will still fall pregnant with well-timed slip matings.

Flirty dirty female

Some females show classic signs of being ready for mating by 'flagging'. This means she holds her tail up and wafts it side to side, so a male catches her scent, but keeps her tail out the way for mating.

She may also 'stand' by freezing her stance, awaiting a male to mount her from behind. 'Lifting' is when she moves her swollen vulva upwards to make it easier for a male dog to penetrate.

It's worth acknowledging some females are 'hormone hungry' and can display these signs even when not fertile, behaving this way too early in their heat or for an overly long and excessive period. Some don't show any signs and are shy and reserved. This means that relying on these signals as an indicator for receptiveness may not be reliable or a fool-proof approach, particularly if the female is a maiden (no previous litters) or doesn't mix with males often.

A female's receptivity to a male can only be taken as a signal that ovulation may have occurred and, therefore, is ready for breeding. Without more in-depth testing, there is no way of truly knowing. This typically means owners will ensure she is covered by the stud within 24 hours of a 'strong stand' and then return 48 hours later, hoping to fertilise the eggs over the biggest possible window of opportunity.

Pick a date in the calendar

I still have some clients who take this approach. On day 1 of the season (the first day of blood), they contact me to pencil in set mating dates in my calendar. I personally find this approach fascinating… these females always manage to ovulate, avoiding vacations, work, weekend commitments and even bank holidays!

Typically these dates are days 11 and 13 of the season. This method means the bitch should be served with two stud covers. Semen commonly lives for 2-3 days inside the female. Two matings 48 hours part will approximately provide a six-day conception opportunity.

By relying on this method, approximately 40% will not conceive. 20% will ovulate before day 11, and 20% will ovulate after day 13, with approximately 60% of bitches ready in this window. I would probably argue it's even less depending on the breed. From my experience, Labradors, the most popular dog in the U.K, are most likely to ovulate between days 12 and 14 of a season and are ready for mating between days 14 and 16. These are a remarkably 'average' ovulating breed.

When a solo litter is confirmed, and the gestational measurements suggest it was due to poor ovulation timing, the sex of the puppy can be predicted. If the mating is too late, it's most likely to be a male puppy; if too early, then more likely to be female.

Some breeders still follow the school of thought that you should breed when the discharge changes from red to a pinky straw colour. I must admit I never really knew what this colour would look like. I should cross-reference it with a Farrow & Ball colour chart.

This rule of thumb is massively flawed. After optimum mating, numerous bitches will still bleed (confirmed with ovulation testing). If the owners waited until the bleeding had stopped, they could have totally missed the fertile window. Discharge can also be impacted by strictures covered in 'Part 3 - The Mating'.

Some breeds do their own thing too; French Bulldogs are renowned for spotting throughout their whole pregnancy, at no detriment to the pregnancy or puppies.

Let's look at what other methods are available on the first rung of the fertility testing ladder.

Low Cost - Some Value Options

The following options are low cost and require some minor assistance to use. I consider them 'do it yourself' techniques and require little knowledge to interpret.

The accuracy of these techniques is unknown due to the lack of credibility that surrounds the products. However, some breeders have committed themselves to these methods and have confidence in their reliability.

These cheap options will require your time to learn the methodology and master the technique. This will take hours of practice, meaning you are exchanging the financial cost of ovulation testing for your time, availability and patience to learn - whilst making possible and naturally expected mistakes during the interim.

The main problem is that developing your eye for such tools can be difficult when you have litters infrequently or are new to breeding. You're going to need to keep highly detailed journals with images, so you can cross-reference, as the mind will easily forget. You could also increase your testing frequency by offering to test others' (friends) dogs. Although these guinea pigs should be totally aware of their participation, in case they wish to use other methods alongside yours.

Placebo Pads

June 2021 celebrated Tupac's 50th birthday if he were alive.

Anyone that knows anything about American Hip-Hop and Rap is aware of the East/West Coast rivalry and how that possibly manifested into the deaths of Tupac and Notorious BIG, who originated from each coast of the States.

My mother's husband, Deen, reckons Tupac faked his death and is still alive.

With that said, Deen loves a conspiracy theory, so I daren't mention 9/11, Area 51 or covid to him either.

Something I do feel is a bit of a conspiracy are Canine Ovulation Test pads.

They seem pretty popular, but that's no doubt because they are super cheap, and the 'testing' can be carried out by the bitch owner. No professional services are required, helping to further reduce expenses and possibly make you feel more in control?

I'm all for proactive breeders, hence why I've written two dog breeding books emphasising the importance of planning and learning to help reduce risk and increase your success rate. I feel these pads are not only a waste of money but, more importantly, when breeding, also a waste of time and could put your breeding plans 6 to 12 months behind schedule.

Now I'm sure some breeders, the manufacturers and marketers will sing from the rooftops about how good they are and report 'never missing a bitch' since using them. But then there's no way of knowing if these bitches would have caught regardless of whether they used these pads or didn't use any testing methods.

You also have to carry out the testing twice a day from day 1 of the season, which means it's a pretty intensive form of testing, considering some people struggle to brush their own teeth twice a day.

The most concerning thing about these 'pads' is there's zero verified evidence of what they do or medical studies on how they work. The user guide advises to mate two days and four days after ovulation. If she ovulates after day 17 of the season, mate consecutively for three days.

This (in my honest opinion) is crazy, eggs don't change their fertility pattern just because they've been released after a particular day in the season. Good quality semen lives for typically 2-3 days, so advising to mate on consecutive days adds little benefit.

I believe the pads are "probably" some form of pH testing strips, and the pH level of the vagina changes as it progresses through a heat cycle? Or with ovulation? I'm not sure, I dunno.

I feel you are putting a lot of faith into 'some chemicals' on a pad that manages to interpret 'a change' and then notify you for pennies.

Interpretation tools, from my experience, have never been great. I've had a written conversation with a native Spanish fellow breeder using Google Translate. Though you can roughly work out what they are referring to, it is not a comprehensive conversation.

I was sent a 'big kiss', so I responded with the same, which then turned into a 'hard kiss' eek, I'm sure that's something else.

Much can be lost in translation, or never seen in the first place. I've also heard of owners struggling to interpret the colour change of these strips, which makes you consider how easy they are to actually use.

Veterinary reproduction specialists don't really acknowledge this testing method, which pretty much shows what they think of them.

Saliva Ovulation Predictor

This is a straightforward tool that helps to magnify saliva crystals to identify 'ferning'. You need to capture some drool from your dog's jowls and allow it to dry.

On investigation, you should see patterns of ferning. This pattern is apparently caused by the electrolytes in saliva, which signifies an increase in oestrogen. Oestrogen stimulates the production of eggs during ovulation, and therefore it may be possible to identify the oestrus phase for mating.

I have never personally used this, so I can't say much more about this method or its reliability.

Higher Cost - Better Value Options

Methods within this band are still owner DIY and require no professional or veterinary assistance. These methods are believed to have around a 3-4 day window of accuracy in pinpointing ovulation.

Draminski

It's a battery-operated handheld probe that must be inserted internally into the bitch's vagina. As far as I'm aware, this equipment was designed initially for mammals that have dry seasons (no blood).

It measures something, but there seems to be no research online to indicate what it measures, or how it indicates ovulation. If you decide to try this product, you need to test the bitch every day of her season and make a note of the levels.

This needs to be plotted so you visually identify a pattern and then can pinpoint ovulation.

I see many of these being 'resold' online from my observation. This indicates that it doesn't work well, or people struggle to commit to testing daily to identify the bitch's ovulation pattern.

The probe is relatively long, approximately 8" and plastic coated with a metal tip, requiring a confident owner whose comfortable with handling dog genitalia. Let alone shoving things in it of this size. I think many would lack the confidence to operate it effectively.

Vaginal cytology

This is the first of the methods we have covered that I can recommend. It's believed to improve ovulation detection from 40% to 65%.

This method does require some initial outlay to purchase the microscope and kit, approximately £350.00. Using a clean swab and confidence to collect vaginal cells. The cells then need to be transferred onto a glass microscope slide and stained. Once stained and dried, they can be viewed under a high magnification microscope.

The epithelium cells that line the vagina respond to oestrogen, a reproductive sex hormone, allowing for a predictable change in the cells' size and shape. Rising oestrogen levels cause the cells to become "cornified" - the cells become large and flattened, with small or absent nuclei.

Think about a kernel of corn from a dried cob. It's all smooth and round, fairly small in size, but the kernels explode open and become popcorn when heated. Much more significant in size, with fluffy edges.

This is the sort of change that happens to vaginal cells. Once they are looking like popcorn, you should breed the female. Again this method is most successful if two matings are 48 hours apart. Cytology also allows for typical and non-typical bacteria to be identified as part of the vaginal flora. Some breeders will put the female on a course of antibiotics as preventative care; I wouldn't consider this necessary unless the female has a previous history of poor conception - then I would opt for a bacterial culturing of a vaginal swab specimen for signs of genital disease at your vets.

If you plan to breed frequently or have a stud dog, I recommend this is a skill worth learning with some investment of time and money. You'll need to develop an eye of observation to understand what you are seeing and keep a detailed log to track your success and challenges.

If you don't have the patience to learn this skill, you may wish to pay for a highly experienced individual with an already trained eye to carry out the cytology for you. This method can be used in conjunction with other methods, such as progesterone ovulation blood testing, to help keep costs manageable.

From my experience, I find cytology more suitable for small to medium-sized breeds. The cells are collected from lower down in the vaginal canal in larger breeds. These may have been shed some time ago, decreasing the accuracy. The bigger the dog, the less accurate I find the cell development due to the limited size of the collection swab.

Highest Cost - Best Value Options

Methods within this band are the highest regarding cost but are also deemed the most accurate. Over the last decade, these methods have become more accessible, meaning you aren't restricted to veterinary or vet laboratory opening hours. There are independent clinics offering dog breeding services and specialising in these methods, providing flexibility on weekends and bank holidays whilst offering other additional breeding services such as artificial insemination.

During the oestrus phase of a heat, the oestrogen hormone stimulates the ovaries to produce eggs. The Luteinizing Hormone (LH)stimulates the ovaries to release the eggs, and Progesterone Hormone is required to maintain a pregnancy and increases rapidly after the LH surge.

Testing for the rise in Progesterone levels can detect that the eggs have been released and are awaiting fertilisation. You can test for the LH level, but you would need to test at least daily to catch the LH surge because the level does not stay elevated like Progesterone. Progesterone testing requires a small amount (1.3ml) of whole blood to be taken from the bitch. This blood is then processed, and the serum tested.

Progesterone testing comes in various guises, and people can become confused with the terminology between them, a bit like referring to a vacuum cleaner as a Hoover. Hoover is a brand name for that particular home appliance.

Premate ovulation testing is a semi-quantitative method originally offered by some vet practices as an 'in house' testing. And Ovucheck Premate is a brand name that can cause some confusion when people refer collectively to progesterone testing as 'Premate'. Practices might also insist you have to buy a complete kit of 6, like a box of eggs, when in reality you could only need one test making this option expensive.

The results are visual and require human interpretation. This can result in less accuracy due to the technician's personal opinion, experience and understanding. This means it's less accurate than quantitative testing, which requires no human interpretation.

This brings us to quantitative "Progesterone testing", which is believed to improve the accuracy of pinpointing ovulation (and hence breeding success) from 65% to 90%. The results are numerically quantifiable and are calculated by a calibrated machine. Meaning there is less misinterpretation or misunderstanding of the results. Some people will refer to this as Premate testing, but that's a brand made for a semi-quantitative method.

Some vet practices may have one of these Progesterone reading machines on-site or use a vet lab and receive the results the same or the next day. Some practices are happy to draw the blood but cannot test it, so you can find your own independent testing facility for rapid results.

The benefits of using an independent clinic, especially if they are offering additional breeder services, are that they generally have a better understanding to advise when to mate, considering additional factors such as stud distance, mating methods, and breed.

Testing should start between days 6 and 9 of the season. I advise people to be prepared to carry out up to three tests. If your female is prone to early ovulation, you'll only need one, average two and late three. If you need more than three, you probably would have never caught that bitch without testing anyway, so consider it money well spent.

You should plan and organise this method well before your female is in season. Have the conversation with your vet, not the receptionist, as it can become a game of Chinese whispers, and the messages can get miscommunicated. Pre-order kits if you plan to post the blood to a Laboratory or Clinic, and if using a local independent clinic, contact them when your female is on day 1 of her season to get a scheduled appointment.

Understanding Progesterone Results

I strongly recommend that you note all the results, including the day of season, date and time, so they can be referred to at any point. You might even want to look back on her past numbers when she's having her second or third litter, as it will help you build a picture of her fertility pattern.

There are two scales (or units) of results for progesterone testing. You must make sure everyone involved with the mating is working on the same scale because reading the numbers on the wrong scale can mean you might mate when you shouldn't and not mate when you should.

The measures are nmol/l or ng/ml. It's a bit like cm and inches.

There are online calculators to convert the figures, but 1 ng = 3.18 nmol, so you can multiply or divide by 3.18 to convert from one scale to the other.

Just remember that ng is the lower scale of the two.

Many online charts advise on what the best progesterone numbers are to breed. These numbers are subject to slight variation due to the machine they have been processed on, the machine manufacture and its own calibration curve.

It's been studied, and now rather than testing to find ovulation, it's believed to be more accurate to use progesterone levels to find the LH surge. Research shows this number is more consistent than using an 'ovulation' number. You would breed 4 days after the LH surge, as the eggs are released 2 days after this surge, so they are then fertile 4 days from the LH peak.

This means it's now advisable to breed 4 days after the result of 2.0-3.0ng (6.4-9.5nmol), rather than the original advice to breed 2 days after 8.0-12.0ng (25+nmol), which 'loosely' confirms ovulation or mate immediately from 18.0ng (57+nmol).

You do not breed on ovulation, as the eggs need to mature. This typically takes 48 hours. This is why regular and methodical testing is necessary, following the testing technician's advice regarding retesting.

If you test a female and she's already 45.0ng and 'technically' anything over 30.0ng, the eggs are already ageing, and it's probably too late to mate. However, if you had tested the female three days before, and she was only 3.0ng (LH surge), the second test 3 days later confirms she has a steep ovulation curve and may have a smaller optimal window than most bitches. She will probably still catch at 45ng as it's less than 4 days from LH surge, so she should still be fertile and covered.

If the female's first test was 45.0ng, we have no idea when her LH surged. She may have ovulated, maybe 3, 5 or even 7 days before. This means if you did breed her, there's a high chance she won't conceive, or if she does, then possibly with a small litter (1 or 2 pups, most probably male).

I strongly advise against 'one off' blood testing as a 'guesstimate'. It's better to test routinely to catch the LH surge and identify ovulation.

Another alternative approach is to cytology test until the cells have cornified and then do one blood test to pinpoint ovulation. Combining these techniques can work well in particular cases and make vigorous ovulation testing more financially feasible, but routine progesterone blood testing would be deemed gold standard and best practice.

The last situation you want to manifest is that you force your female to be bred naturally at the incorrect point of her season because you failed to ovulation test. Not just the lack of success, but this is distressing for her physically but also mentally.

Second Fear Phase (Socialisation)

Many breeders know the importance of puppy socialisation and its long-term impact on a dog's mental well-being. The window is typically around 5 weeks old and between 8 to 14 weeks. There is also a second fear phase when a dog is around 6 to 14 months of age and is linked to a dog's sexual maturity and growth spurts.

Reactivity levels rise during this window, causing a dog to act defensively, and become protective and more territorial. Owners tend to observe fears that seem to materialise from nowhere. This is a time to avoid traumatic experiences, and forcing a breeding could be considered in this category.

Encouraging a breeding at the wrong time could make subsequent breedings much more difficult for that particular female.

Progesterone testing removes all the guesswork and is my preferred method due to its accuracy. It will save you money and time on requiring multiple matings and should result in bigger litters. While providing a more accurate due date, fewer matings are required because ovulation and optimal fertility were correctly identified.

Testing will also help you identify silent/dry seasons. You'll typically require 1-2 tests to confirm if a bitch is in season or not. The first half of the split season is non-ovulating, so it would be unproductive if you mated her during this time.

Pregnancy

A canine pregnancy is typically 9 weeks, 63 days from ovulation. People get confused and think it's 63 days from mating, putting you two days out. If you did not ovulation test, you could be working with a due date that may be one week out. In this instance, gestational measures of the foetal sac or skull during the ultrasound pregnancy scan will help narrow the due date window. Identifying ovulation through testing can help you plan for a more accurate birthing date and schedule your elective section should you need one.

Reverse progesterone testing is when you carry out the same progesterone test, but you are looking for a low number of results. The drop in progesterone level (which must stay elevated to maintain a pregnancy) drops when the pups are ready for delivery. A result of 5.0-8.0ng (15.9-25.4nmol) suggests that a c-section the following day won't compromise the puppies, and the female should not labour overnight. Under 5.0ng confirms the female is really for a c-section.

Some breeders prefer the elective section to safeguard the bitch's delivery whilst ensuring she has the best possible veterinary care and support by avoiding weekends and bank holidays. This proactive approach may be considered unnecessary for some breeders and too controlling for some vets. It's one of the few ways a breeder can ensure the puppies have the best viability and the dam the safest delivery. Knowing a female's reverse progesterone levels is vital if you plan to take this approach.

I've also had breeders use reverse testing for natural whelping to help pinpoint when labour may start. An XL American Bully, Solo, had whelped her previous litter of 13 puppies early, and her pregnancy scan measures suggested this too. Her breeder was unsure if she would do the same for her second litter. She was reversed tested on day 60 gestation and was 21.0ng, suggesting labour was at least 48 hours away. True to form, she started labour around 50 hours later, 62 days from ovulation.

Reverse testing is also helpful if first stage labour stalls. This stage can last up to 36 hours, so testing will provide beneficial information on the best course of action and help avoid unnecessary or early c-sections.

Chapter 7 - Ovulation detection summary

During this chapter, we have covered:

- How ovulation testing is critical for breeding success.
- Reviewing the plethora of ovulation testing methods available and the specific value of each approach for increasing success.
- The additional benefits of Progesterone ovulation testing, and how to correctly interpret the results.

CHAPTER 8
Sourcing a Stud Dog

I asked on my social media, "How do you find a good stud dog?" it seems a pretty straightforward question but pretty tricky to answer.

Most people suggested research through:

- Existing Bloodline and Pedigree
- Dog shows, Link-Ups & Dog meets
- Breed Club Journals, Website & Health testing schemes
- Breeding Announcements/Advertisements
- Showcasing platforms, e.g. Champdogs or Pets4Homes
- Word of mouth
- Google

In short, there is no right or wrong way to find a stud dog. The more extensive your canine network, the more exposed to possibilities you'll be. For this reason, online platforms unquestionably come into their own for this benefit. Beware, plenty of images are manipulated to make a dog look better than reality, and videos can be cleverly edited, so I always recommend you see the dog in the flesh before the mating - to decide if he is 'the one' for you.

Stud Viewings

So it's somewhat a minefield, but as already emphasised, health should be of the utmost importance. Don't just believe the ticked 'Health Check' box on a stud advertisement. Ensure you see all certificate copies before making decisions. Pictures and videos are great, but there's nothing better than seeing the dog in the flesh. You'll pick up on much more than just the dog's conformation and temperament. When seen in his home environment, it'll also inform you of the owner's level of care and attention to maintaining the dog.

You'll be able to have direct conversations about the quality of pups he has sired and what they consider excellent or high quality to be. Some stud owners may consider a coat colour or markings of the highest importance, others health and others conformation. Hopefully, you'll find a stud owner striving for the same goals as you, and they are forthcoming with breed knowledge and advice, so they can support you during your female's pregnancy and once the pups are born.

I have an outstanding client, Diana Stevens of Wylanbriar Labradors, that I feel all stud owners should aspire to be. She has a large, varied and expansive, health tested 'rotating' stud team. As a return visitor, you'll always find a male suitable for your female. Di maintains an impressive website full of supportive breeding information and actively manages a Facebook Group. The online space creates a community of like-minded owners who can ask specific questions related to mating, pregnancy, whelping, rearing, weaning or homing puppies.

Pretty fabulous, eh? And to top it off, she actively updates the website with expected and confirmed litters and contact details. Her reputation sells your pups for you, subject to your own new owner vetting.

Di is most certainly at the top of the field in what she offers, and I believe other stud owners' expectations should be just as high.

Outside of the U.K

Don't limit your thinking to dogs only available in the U.K, or whatever country you are domicile in. I mention later in this book the stud I found on social media. I drove to Holland to view him in advance of the breeding. Later that year, I returned to collect and chill semen, which was inseminated 2 days later.

Part 3 - 'The Mating' covers all options available to you, but it's pretty easy to have chilled semen sent to you from most of Europe and far as America. Brexit and the Pandemic have added a few additional complexities that weren't previously an issue. It's manageable if the stud owner's fertility clinic is experienced, a suitable courier is used, and the sourced clinic on your end is experienced with waking and warming chilled semen for insemination. You most certainly should consider it an option for you.

Breeding Tools

Estimated Breeding Values - EBV 's

Some tools can help you decide who may be the best possible suitor for your female. Depending on the pedigree registry, for example, the Kennel Club have online facilities through MyKC (breed dependant) for you to 'try and test' before breeding particular dogs.

Firstly you have the **KC Estimated breeding values (EVBs)** for hip and elbow dysplasia. EBVs estimate a dog's risk of developing certain health conditions and how they may be affected. A dog's EBV score will always be calculated concerning the breed average (always set at zero). Dogs with a higher than average risk of passing on genes for hip/elbow dysplasia will have an EBV higher than zero i.e. a positive number, e.g. 10. The higher the number, the greater the risk.

Dogs with a lower than average genetic risk of hip/elbow dysplasia will have an EBV lower than zero i.e. a negative number, e.g. -10. The lower the number, the less the risk. A dog's EBV can change during its lifetime, either upward or downward, as more information becomes available either about the dog itself or its relatives.

At birth, a puppy's EBV will be the average of its parents' EBVs, e.g. a sire with an EBV of -5 and a dam with an EBV of +5 will produce a litter of puppies with an EBV of 0.

Inbreeding Coefficient - COI 's

COI stands for Coefficient of Inbreeding. It measures the common ancestors of a dam and sire and indicates the probability of how genetically similar they are.

Dogs within an individual breed are genetically similar, e.g. a Labrador to Labrador breeding. Some breeds have their own COI. For example, the Kennel Club using up to 26 generations, has determined that the breed average COI for a Labrador is 6.6%.

Spice, my chocolate Labrador which I bought recently, has a COI of 11.9%. This is higher than the breed average, so she is more 'inbred' than the ideal average Labrador due to some of her ancestors sharing the same genetic material.

This typically happens when a breeder decides to 'line breed' a dog's pedigree to keep and maintain particular characteristics of a bloodline. This is a dog's phenotype, and includes characteristics like height, eye colour and coat texture.

The problem with continual line breeding, which will increase the COI, is that you start to double up on both the genetically good and bad material. The previously recessive, unrecognised traits will become evident as you double up on similar DNA. These recessive genes may have associated health issues that could negatively impact an entire litter.

For this reason, most registries will no longer register close breedings, such as Father/Daughter, Mother/Son or full Brother/Sister as the COI would be 25%.

It's recommended that the COI is kept as low as possible and it is possible to achieve lower than the Breed average (if there is one). Many show breeders attempt to juggle COI's to try and keep physical type whilst maintaining health. Subsequently, some would be happy to agree to a Grandfather/granddaughter mating, half-brother/sister, or Uncle/Niece, typically 12.5%. They should then consider 'out crossing' on the next generation to bring the COI back down.

From my experience, line breeding is fine when you have a good knowledge of the bloodline, but research and knowledge are fundamental for any of these breeding decisions.

Don't be fooled that a low breeding COI will result in healthy pups. Each breeding dog must also be assessed for health issues and compatibility as a breeding pair. Even if both dam and sire are totally unrelated and a 0% COI is achieved, they could still pass affected genes to their offspring - producing unhealthy puppies.

There are websites where you can calculate the inbreeding of future puppies produced by two potential mates. Alternatively, using an empty pedigree template and completing it for a mock litter will help you visually identify any common ancestors.

Chapter 8 - Sourcing a stud summary

During this chapter, we have covered:

- The considerations to be made when sourcing a suitable stud dog.
- Available opportunities to use a dog outside of the UK.
- How to use breeding tools to find the most suitable breeding combination.

Part 1 - The Bitch Summary

We've covered an immense amount of information, and this book is Part 1 heavy as the female is vital to the success of your planned litter.

Do you still want to breed after reading these chapters?

You are officially passionate about dogs, it's apparent you've got the dog breeding itch, and you want to scratch it. You seem curious, which is rarely a bad thing.

You should now appreciate how vital the female is to rearing strong, healthy puppies. We've looked at every aspect of a female's reproductive ability from her health, including genetics, conformation and temperament, to how you should be best informed of this information to find the best possible mating partner and stud for her.

We've looked extensively at the reproductive cycle, why it's essential to your breeding success, and how to navigate it to your benefit with various available ovulation testing options.

I pulled back the covers on the realistic costs associated with breeding and what funds need to be available regardless of the success of the litter. Finally, we've looked at what you need to do before breeding your female to ensure she's in peak condition to rear a litter and what you can do to help stack the odds in your favour.

Acknowledging and accepting this information should put you in good stead to breed your female safely, reducing any risks by being better informed about your choices and, more importantly, why you have decided.

In the coming chapters, we'll consider the challenges of dog breeding - the less glamorous stuff not many talk about.

Want more help?

While reading books for insight and knowledge is great, they don't offer real-time support because they are written months, if not years in advance, of you reading them. This means they may or may not answer a specific question or provide support on a situation you are experiencing.

For this reason, I've decided to build a community called the Home Breeder Hub, where like-minded proactive owners can congregate and collaborate. Sharing any current issues and challenges they may be experiencing. Do you:

- Still have a specific question about breeding your female?
- Believe that reading this book has prompted more detailed and relevant questions?
- Have a complex or difficult female that has already failed to conceive, and keen to get it right next time?
- Feel like you are running out of time? Have only one last chance to get your female in pup?

Then the Home Breeder Hub may be for you.

Regardless of if you are new to breeding, an occasional breeder or feeling pretty competent, everyone likes to know there's someone that's got their back. In the Hub, I'm available to support and advise you, co-cry with you and share your successes. We all need reassurance as breeding can sometimes feel isolating and daunting.

Home Breeder Hub - Very Important Breeder (ViB) Access

The Home Breeder Hub is a paid monthly membership for the conscientious dog owner, who I like to call ViB's, Very Important Breeders. This is a fabulous community of breeders who want to raise the bar and seek reliable support and advice. The Hub is the only way you'll have direct access to me, so I can support you on your breeding journey and experiences. If you are dedicated to investing in this pastime, then the Hub is the place for you.

What do you get as a ViB?

- Fortnightly online breeding support sessions offering an opportunity for you to discuss your dog's specific breeding needs and issues - ***Value £197***
- Monthly breeding educational webinars including guest speakers - ***Value £97***
- Quarterly printed and posted publication straight to your letterbox - ***Value £97***
- Unlimited access to all resources within the Hub - ***Priceless!***
- Access to the community forum for more in-depth doggy discussions - ***Value £97***

Book reader offer for you

You can register for the Home Breeder Hub and claim your first month for just **£9.99** by going to **www.caninefamilyplanner.com/DSVIB**

- PART TWO: The Stud -

CHAPTER 9

Stud Duties & Expectations

I know I said in the preface that each part of this book could be read individually, but I strongly recommend any stud owner should read Part 1 - 'the Bitch', it will help you understand the bitch owner's perspective and appreciate why they ask, act and behave as they do.

We all know the theory of men being from Mars and women being from Venus, I'm sure it's no different for dog breeding. From my observation, most breeders are female, and stud owners are more likely to be male. So as a stud owner, you'll need to be able to communicate effectively with all types of people and personalities.

Pizza-man Peter

In 2012 I was invited to judge a dog show in Italy, I graciously accepted the appointment and enjoyed my four day trip to Parma, the home of aptly named Parma Ham and Parma Cheese.

I've always found Italian hospitality to be outstanding. On one of the days, the host asked the judging panel what we fancied for dinner that evening. One of the judges asked if it was possible to visit an authentic Pizzeria. After much discussion between the Italians (I've learnt even if it seems a heated conversation by their mannerisms, it never is), we were informed it was possible, but it was a 30 minute drive.

That evening we found the restaurant thanks to my satnav (I had hired a car), rather than the host's natural geography or navigation skills.

We settled in and were given menus, the usual restaurant protocol.

Having eaten at Pizza Express, a nationwide Italian authentic Pizzeria founded in 1965, I thought I'd go for a Pollo ad Astra - toppings including chicken, sweet red peppers, red onion and Cajun spices. The Italian hosts looked at me, confused.

"Chicken? On a pizza?" they asked.

"Yes, please."

"We'll have to ask the chef."

The chef refused to put chicken on a pizza, apparently, that is sacrilege.

Who'd have thought it?

An "authentic" Italian (if a little commercialised) U.K restaurant seems not to be selling authentic pizzas. With a bit of research, the Founder of Pizza Express, Peter Boizot, is 'actually' English, but did work in Europe for ten years. Not quite the same.

This same kind of deception can also come with owning a stud dog. Being a stud dog owner and offering your dog should be taken seriously. It looks like an easy service to offer from a distance, but the more you look into it, the more it may not seem to be the case.

When your dog is getting paid for a service, it's your responsibility to ensure the bitch and owner receive the best possible authentic support and advice that she's mated safely with success.

You can feel under extreme pressure when publicly offering your dog because you'll be working within a time-bound situation. There is nothing more frustrating than not being able to mate two dogs, given that it's meant to be a natural thing.

It's naive to think that two dogs can just run around the garden, mate and tie within 15 minutes with little distress or drama.

As a stud owner, you will need some kind of process or protocol so all bitch owners receive the same service from you.

If you're looking to handle your own dog, I recommend that you seek support from someone more experienced to show you, teach and train you how to do this safely.

Or elicit the help of someone experienced to help if your attempts fail, a Plan B if you will. It would be ideal if this person also had experience with artificial insemination.

Stud Owner Roles & Responsibilities

Some key aspects you should plan, so the mating goes smoothly include:

- Ensuring your dog has good fertility
- Suitably vetting the bitch
- Health testing your male
- Providing a stud dog contract
- Understanding ovulation testing and its benefits
- Supervising the mating
- Handling the bitch to ensure a safe mating
- Ensuring the dogs are safe once tied so that neither dog is hurt or injured
- Assisting or advising if the bitch shows little interest in mating
- Being available to give advice to the bitch owner with pregnancy, whelping and puppy care
- Willing to help with any puppy problems, i.e. health issues that may be hereditary or congenital
- Assist them with selling and placing puppies

I'm sure you'll agree it's an expansive list. Agreeing to use your dog on a bitch that is not well matched may impact the puppies produced and, ultimately, your dog's reputation.

It is your responsibility to ensure that the mating between the two dogs is justified and the mating will be beneficial to the breed and the larger canine community.

Can any dog be offered at stud?

Within reason, yes, but in reality, will anyone want to use 'any old' dog?

The dog needs to have desirable traits or assets for anyone to wish to use him and, even more so, to pay to use him. If you consider buying a puppy with future plans to offer him at stud, you could be in uncertain territory. No one has a crystal ball. Even if the parents are extensively health tested, from desired bloodlines, with impeccable temperaments, there are no biological guarantees that the puppy you pick will follow suit.

Buying a Puppy Stud

There are so many phases a dog will advance through from a puppy to full maturity, which means there are so many places for it to go wrong. You could end up hugely disappointed if you purchase a puppy with the solid intent to stud and fails to make the grade. You'll have little opportunity to recoup any initial costs and expenses, but even more so, the time you've invested waiting for him to mature.

You'll also need to factor in where you envisage the stud demand in two years. Just because a particular trait is popular now, there may not be the same level of interest going forward.

If you haven't bred the puppy and plan to buy from another Breeder, you'll need to ensure the puppy has the correct ownership levels. These should be full Breeding papers, with no endorsements or the sale contract detailing restrictions or special conditions.

Purchasing an Adult Stud

When looking to buy a horse, you can request a Pre-purchase examination (PPE), before any full commitments are made. The PPE is carried out by a vet and consists of 5 stages. The vet will provide a written report to the prospective buyer, and the buyer accepts the conditions and implications when purchasing the horse or not. There is no such thing for buying an adult dog, but maybe there should be? The best you'll receive is a vet health check (see Part 1 - Physical Health), so you could still be kept in the dark about many things.

If you plan to purchase an adult stud, you must be cautious and ensure the animal is thoroughly health tested, including fertility checks with two descended testicles, DNA tests, eye examinations, hip and elbow scoring and any other relevant breed-related testing with a sound temperament. It's unusual when older breeding males are available, so you'll need to be sure the reason he has become available is genuine.

If you already have a male of breeding age, who you would like to offer at stud and fulfils the above criteria, you should certainly read on.

Male Credentials

If you plan to offer your male at public stud, it's recommended to have a semen evaluation. The evaluation should be completed within 3 months of you planning to use him (due to semen growing in a 3 month cycle). Typically many will have the first assessment between 9 to 12 months.

Macro checks - Low detail

If you plan to handle your own stud dog with little testing equipment, a macro overview check of a dog is possible once collected. You'll gain an idea of the amount/volume he's produced. Leave this to stand for 8 hrs, and you'll see the spermatozoa sink.

This will give you an idea of the concentration, the greater the volume of sunken white mass, the better.

Even a simple check of his testicle size is a reasonable indicator of sexual maturity, paired with the dog's general libido and behaviour at home.

Micro checks - High detail

Micro-level detailed checks, completed by an experienced eye such as a canine reproduction expert or fertility clinic, will provide a detailed breakdown of information regarding the collection and its concentration. For example, 150 million per ml of spermatozoa, with good motility (how well it swims) and low abnormality rate (the sperm structure), would be considered a good sample. We basically want a sperm equivalent of Olympic gold medallist Michael Phelps.

Should any of the above qualities not achieve 'good' status, you may wish to consider delaying offering him at public stud and retesting him in 3 months once the dog has been given a supplement of zinc and vitamin E, especially if the male is young.

Stud Viewings

Bitch owners may want to view the male in the flesh before the mating, enquiring about any offspring or related dogs. Stud viewings take time, prompting an online profile with some high-quality images and videos, copies of his health certificates and relevant documentation, so people can do some research for themselves (or be ready to email them copies). Be sure to edit the documents by removing his registration details and your address from the public domain. Embark, a DNA testing Laboratory, offer a platform in which you can upload this information easily.

Discuss with the bitch owner in advance their expectations for mating, stud cost and availability. Preferably have this detailed and finalised in a stud contract.

Managing Availability

You should ask the bitch owner to contact you the first day they see blood, confirming Day 1 of her season. It's becoming more common for stud owners to request that any females are ovulation tested. This prevents the stud from being overused, covering females that aren't yet in the optimal fertility window, especially if the stud is busy, meaning less unnecessary breedings. Bitches seem to start cycles with significant weather changes, meaning a multiple number of females may need covering in a reasonably short period.

Ovulation testing will ease the stress of identifying the optimal breeding window for new or novice breeders, maiden dogs and difficult bitches. Depending on the ovulation method chosen, the bitch owner will be advised when to mate and how long you should wait between the first and second matings.

It is possible for a healthy well-proven stud dog to cover two bitches on the same day. Acting in and practising good faith, all parties should be aware of this, and by no means should it be considered typical or frequent practice. There are now additional techniques to assist with clash matings, such as collecting from the male and splitting the collection, especially if you are confident of his fertility status. This enables you to cover two (or more) females if all are present simultaneously, or the latter female's collection can be chilled. You'll need assistance from someone who has the equipment to process the collection, such as a canine fertility clinic. If you plan to handle your own dog, you can learn yourself, but you will need in advance the correct equipment and invest significant time and money to learn the process.

Chilling a semen collection can also add flexibility to a situation. The stud may not be readily available due to either party's limited diary availability or unexpected emergencies. I once chilled a collection from a Labrador who was due to have his anterior cruciate ligament (ACL) repaired after a fall into a frozen pond on a shoot, the same day a bitch was ready to be covered. She was inseminated once with the chilled collection and successfully whelped and reared seven puppies.

Boarding Bitches

I do not recommend boarding bitches for breeding due to potential liability with care. If the bitch owner has ovulation tested, then there is no need. If they haven't tested and requested a natural mating, they may expect you to board their bitch.

At this time, you want the bitch to be most settled and stress-free; leaving her in an alien environment is far from ideal, even in the perfect home and being pampered. The bitch may not be anxious, but she's still super hormonal whilst staying in foreign surroundings.

Along with the reality that if you happen to board more than one female at any one time, the interactions between two hormonal dogs that aren't familiar could have much more severe repercussions.

Natural Mating vs Artificial Insemination

It will be worth having the conversation in advance with the bitch owner regarding what method of mating they favour.

Artificial Insemination (AI) is ideal for immature, timid or inexperienced males, dominant bitches or a stud with physical difficulties from injury or age.

The Kennel Club now approves non-surgical (intra-vaginal) AI, where semen is placed directly into the vaginal canal. AI tends to be a much quicker, less stressful and faster process. It also means the quality of the collection can be checked before insemination if needed. If you decide to take this route when the pups are pedigree registered, the KC suggest that form 2 is completed confirming insemination details by all parties, including the person who conducted the AI. You'll need to check with other alternative registries for the requirements they may stipulate upon such methods.

Natural matings should always be assisted; a tie (two dogs locking together) isn't required for a mating to be successful, though most bitch owners prefer it. Ovulation testing can impact the number of matings that may be required. Traditionally with no ovulation testing, you are advised to mate, miss a day and mate again. This covers the largest ovulation window possible from first mating to 2-3 days after the last, totalling nearly 6 days.

When cytology is the ovulation testing method (full details in Part 1 - Ovulation detection), it's recommended to follow this pattern. When progesterone blood testing is chosen, one mating should be enough, ideal for dogs that aren't local and you need to travel for. Should you wish for a second mating, it should be within 24-48 hours, no later, as the eggs will only be ageing, depending on her specific blood results.

The Breeding Combination

It can be arduous for bitch owners to find a suitable stud, and there is much planning and preparation before his assistance is even required. Bitch owners will have varying reasons and motivations to breed, this will be reflected in their choice of the stud.

Some aspects of the stud should always be essential criteria, including their current health, breed-specific tests and relevant virtues and faults they hold.

As part of the breeding, you should never want to double up on the same fault or issues. For example, if the mating pair had eye conditions, poor hips or DNA carriers of the same hereditary health condition, they should not be bred together.

You want a beautifully fitting pair - like two jigsaw puzzle pieces. At this point, you, the stud owner, need to be the gatekeeper of the acceptability of the breeding. You need to vet the female and owner to have confidence in the quality of puppies the breeding pair will make. When two dogs are paired, the following should be considered:

- **Bitch Age & Breeding History** - Stud owners should be asking for copies of any registration paperwork to confirm age. She must be at least 12 months and under 8 years old. Research if she has previously reared litters, when and at what intervals considering the number of puppies in each litter. The overall condition of the female should be considered, a bitch under or overweight will find carrying a litter more challenging and could possibly compromise the puppies or even be life-threatening for herself.

- **Health Tests & Results incl. DNA** - Stud owners should be asking if the female has had any relevant breed health testing and if the results are suitable for the paired male. If the female has not been tested, the stud owner should educate and encourage the female to be tested before breeding. If your male is a carrier or affected on any relevant DNA tests, then you should decline the female if she is also affected or carrier - as affected puppies can be produced.

- **Breed Conformation -** Stud owners should be looking to breed only with structurally sound females. Not only due to potential problems that may be passed to the puppies, but she should be able to safely, comfortably carry and rear a litter. There should be no obvious or noticeable physical awkwardness such as lameness, weak joints or apparent injury or damage.

- **Breed Type** - There are subtle differences between dogs within a breed, which means different 'breed types' can form. Typically this is forged from a prolific breeder who bred and kept some key traits or characteristics over generations; these then become a feature of the kennel that people would then consider a family resemblance. Breeding similar breed types will help maintain consistency of the litter quality. Similar breed types don't necessarily mean the same bloodline or pedigree, but the inbreeding coefficient should still be considered.

- **Temperament** - The female should have a neutral and balanced personality and reacts well in various situations. It should be encouraged that only well-natured dogs are bred. A well-balanced temperament can improve upon a reactive temperament, but two extreme temperaments (aggressive or shyness)should not be bred together.

Some tools can help you visualise the compatibility of two breeding dogs, guiding you to make informed decisions before agreeing to the breeding.

- **Coefficient of inbreeding (COI) -** This information is covered in detail under Part 1 - 'The Bitch, Sourcing a Stud under Breeders Tools', so I recommend you read that section.

In short, COI measures the number of common ancestors of a dam and sire and indicates the probability of how genetically similar they are. Ideally, the lower the COI, the less genetic material the parents share, so the less likely any recessive DNA will be doubled up… in very simple terms, a high COI may produce previously unknown health issues. For this reason, most registries will no longer register close breedings, such as Father/Daughter, Mother/Son or full Brother/Sister as the COI would be 25%.

- **KC Estimated breeding values (EVBs)** again, this information is covered in detail under Part 1 - 'The Bitch, Sourcing a Stud under Breeders Tools', so I recommend you read that section.

EBVs estimate a dog's risk of developing hip and elbow dysplasia conditions and how they may be affected. A dog's EBV score will always be calculated concerning the breed average. Dogs with a higher than average risk of passing on genes will have an EBV higher than zero. The higher the number, the greater the risk. At birth, a puppy's EBV will be the average of its parents' EBVs, e.g. a sire with an EBV of -5 and a dam with an EBV of +5 will produce a litter of puppies with an EBV of 0.

Research what possible breed-related tests are available, some will be a simple DNA swab, whilst others may require you to take the dog to be assessed by a professional. Full details are in 'Part 1 - The Bitch, Physical Health & Mental Health'.

You must remember that potential future puppy owners are becoming more educated about health. Making bitch owners more critical with their stud selection and requirements. Bitch owners are looking for studs with good credentials because this will help them sell their puppies.

Breeding Age

If your dog is unproven, there are a few basic checks that even the most unqualified person should participate in if you plan to handle your own dog. The details will be covered in Part 3 - Mating.

Most registries won't have a minimum age limit for the male to sire a litter. Most breeders would advise 12 months old, as they should be sexually mature and mentally adaptable to the practice. Most males have reached maturity by 2 years old and produce optimal semen samples until 7 years old. Males can only fertilise the number of eggs released by the female, so he's not fully accountable for a litter size unless his fertility is below standard, meaning he doesn't fertilise every available egg, reducing the potential litter size.

Chapter 9 - Stud duties and expectations summary

During this chapter, we have covered:

- The expectations and associated responsibilities of being a stud dog owner.
- The basic requirements and credentials to offer a male at public stud.
- The importance of checking the compatibility of two breeding dogs including age, health, conformation, breed type and temperament.

CHAPTER 10

Stud Contracts

Documenting this information may feel 'overkill', but you are offering a paid service, and it's sensible to collate relevant information to prevent any future misunderstandings. This ensures all parties are on the same page with the exact expectations.

Both parties should document and sign any agreements regarding the stud fee, terms and conditions before the breeding.

Alongside the contract, you should provide a copy of any of the stud's credentials, including health certificates, DNA results and pedigree. Payment terms may vary if the stud is unproven or charged a handling fee instead of a traditional stud fee. A handling fee is paid at the time of first mating, then the outstanding stud fee on the production of live pups or within a certain number of days of the puppies being born.

Both parties should sign the contract and retain a copy each, which should be kept safe and referred to if needed. Contracts are needed regardless of the type or level of breeding you are involved with.

The terms and conditions of a mating do not fall within the jurisdiction of a registry body, so any breeding terms or stud fees should be arranged by mutual agreement before the mating takes place.

You may also need to consider different contracts depending on the type of breeding that is planned, a dog-to-dog 'natural' breeding or an AI are the most common forms of breeding. You may have to construct a different contract if you provide chilled semen and frozen semen, particularly when shipments can be delayed due to couriers compromising the collection, rather than direct stud owner liability.

What should you include in the contract?

- **Identification of each dog** - Both dogs should be identified by their registry name and microchip number and be listed in the paperwork. You should also include the date of birth of the dogs. The females should be no younger than 12 months and not exceeding 8 years, males ideally a minimum 12 months old due to sexual maturity (or at least has been fertility tested)

  .
- **Stud Fee** - What is the total amount payable, and when is it due? Any breedings where the stud fee is not paid in full at the time of breeding will involve an element of trust. Another consideration is the stud fee of an unproven stud; maybe this is offered at a discount or delayed payment until puppies are born, or the female is confirmed in pup.

Handling Fee

Some stud owners will offer a handling fee to cover the time and resources needed to conduct the mating and will not charge a stud fee until the bitch is confirmed in pup by ultrasound or when live pups are born.

Pup Back agreement

Other alternative agreements may include 'pup back' arrangements, where the stud owner will receive a puppy in exchange for a stud fee. The contract should detail what pick it will be, at what age the pick is made and possibly the sex. If the stud owner plans to sell the puppy directly on, they must be aware of Lucy's Law if a breeding licence is held. In this scenario, the stud owner would be deemed a third party seller and since April 2020, puppies should only be purchased directly from the Breeder.

Conditions

You'll need to fine-tune some details of what is considered 'a litter', some would argue that one live puppy is a litter, others would say two or even three puppies constitute a litter and what breeding rights they may have.

Traditionally when a bitch owner pays a stud fee, they pay for the service, not puppies. Some stud owners will insist on a quick semen evaluation during AI's before the bitch is inseminated. This means all parties know the collection quality before insemination to rule out any concerns.

Fees will be dependent on your breed, the rule of thumb used to be the cost of a puppy, but in some breeds, puppies now sell well in excess of the stud fee. You'll need to research what's appropriate for you and your dog, including pedigree, popularity, health checks and reputation.

- **Number of Matings** - the number of matings you agree to honour; typically, this is two per season.

- **Remate Opportunities** - the contract should detail what happens if the bitch does not conceive. Typically the stud would offer a repeat mating on her next season if the stud fee has been paid in full. If only a handling fee, then a 'no charge' remate is not expected. It would be suggested they either pay another handling fee or use an entirely different stud dog. You may wish to detail if the remate can be used on another bitch, as the bitch owner may have a situation where there's now a more suitable female for the breeding than the initial. Would you be happy with this? This level of detail should be in the paperwork as potentially it is considered a form of 'stud credit'.

- **Expectations of Puppies** - You may wish to advise the breeder of your expectations that should be met in the rearing of puppies that are sired by your dog. This could be simple husbandry, such as puppies should be vet checked before placed in their new homes, they should be 8 weeks of age and offered free puppy insurance. Maybe that new owners should be suitability vetted and a sales contract completed with diet details and record of worming and weight. If registered, you may wish to state the registration level and if any endorsements or restrictions should be applied to the pups, especially if any have recognised conditions, illness, or even if they should even be registered at all.

Stud Management

There maybe be additional precautions you need to take, over and above the usual pet care, when you are offering your dog at stud. Keeping your dog in the best physical condition will go a long way to improving his desirability and success rate.

Maintaining Fertility

If your male is siring puppies at least every 3 months, then there is little need to monitor his fertility as it will be evident with the females he covers and the number of puppies he's siring. The age at which a male's fertility decreases depends on the individual dog. If the dog is frequently used, they can easily have no negative changes at 8, even 10 years old. Once a male becomes a veteran at 7 years old, if they aren't frequently siring litters, they should be fertility tested before being used.

Typically with ageing males, the semen concentration is still good, so a macro level check looks fine. The problem is that generally, the abnormality rate increases and those abnormal sperm cannot fertilise the eggs. Abnormal morphology such as no tail, curly tails or crooked necks means they can't swim effectively to the egg.

Suppose a dog has been semen checked and the collection was poor, regardless of age. In that case, the dog should be taken for a vet check to identify any possible underlying health conditions impacting his fertility. Some medicines can negatively impact semen quality, so always check if given meds.

External factors like excessive swimming in heated hydro pools, grooming drying cabinets, sweltering weather and males sunbathing or laying on hot flooring (including underfloor heating) can negatively impact semen quality.

The testes are on the outside of the body, so they remain cooler than the body, all the examples above will increase their temperature and possibly impact spermatogenesis (the process of sperm transitioning from germ cells in the testis).

After a failed or poor semen analysis, the environment should be managed, and the relevant supplements provided. The dog should then be rechecked in 3 months. If there is no improvement in the collection, you may need to consider the dog being withdrawn from service.

Improving Collections

It's unnecessary to conduct a 'clean out' collection from a male before breeding unless there is previous knowledge that this may be beneficial. It should be a week before the anticipated planned breeding if you decide to.

Along with 'stud supplements', there are other ways to improve a collection when inseminated. Semen extenders can improve the 'performance' of the collected semen.

Extenders won't fix any 'broken' sperm, but can help the healthy ones by making their environment much more favourable. Semen extenders are mixed with the collection at body temperature and then inseminated into the bitch. They are a concoction of sugars and proteins that provide energy and help allude toxins to help the sperm live longer and travel to and fertilise an egg.

Good quality semen in a suitable bitch is said to live around 2-3 days, but poor quality collections can be boosted to these levels with Semen extenders. Semen extenders are fine to use if there is a legitimate reason. An extender would be good to use on a bitch that's being mated slightly early due to other commitments or calendar clashes. It's also good to use for younger or older stud dogs. The extender shouldn't be used 'just because'. Using an extender on a healthy dog and bitch could result in uncomfortably large litters that could be detrimental to the bitch's health during pregnancy.

Canine STD's

Thankfully canine sexually transmitted diseases (STD's) are pretty rare. But having some general awareness of them will help you understand any potential fertility issues you may experience or at least provide you with some basic details to have a conversation with your vet.

- **Canine herpes virus (CHV)**- It's different to human herpes, although from the same family. It's not fatal to many adults dogs but is hazardous for newborn puppies. It can be transmitted through mating, inhaling the virus through coughs or sneezes, drinking from a contaminated bowl, or sniffing or licking a dog shedding the virus.

  Puppies commonly contract the virus from their mothers, so Dams can be given the vaccine 2 weeks after mating and 2 weeks before they are due to whelp to protect the puppies. There's much debate about how effective the vaccine is. It seems to be an ongoing supply issue with rumours that it may be withdrawn from the market due to the big question mark over its efficacy and the observation that its rare puppy loss is actually diagnosed with herpes.

- **Brucellosis** - is a bacterial infection that can cause fertility issues for any infected dog. It's hazardous for puppies and spreads through mating and contact with infected bodily fluids. Puppies can contract it from their mother during birth. It typically causes inflamed reproductive organs, including the scrotum. Dogs can be blood tested and treated with antibiotics; however, a dog infected should be considered infected for life and neutered to decrease the shedding of the organism. Thankfully it's a rare disease, but it is transmissible to humans.

- **Canine transmissible venereal tumours (CTVTs)**- This is the only transmissible cancer in mammals. Tumours may be seen on the genitals, mouth or nose. Mating can transmit the disease plus by licking, biting or sniffing a tumour. Not to be confused with Papillomas (CPV-1), which are growths or warts due to an immature or suppressed immune system often seen in puppies around their mouth and nose.

Stud Supplements

You first need to be realistic with the capability of what any stud supplements can achieve, as some poor fertility will be due to bodily degeneration, such as ageing. Vitamins and minerals are essential to help a body function and repair.

Supplements may need to be given to help boost the body's system should the diet not provide the complete requirements or the life stage/age alters, causing a deficit. Supplementations take at least 3 months to be metabolised into the body's system.

A small number of supplements can be given to proactive studs. The first is wheat germ oil which includes polyunsaturated fats; linoleic acid (omega-6) and alpha-linolenic acid (omega-3) - antioxidants for the reproductive organs and remove harmful free radicals formed as a by-product of everyday body metabolism. Vitamin E has also been proven to increase pregnancy and birth rates. I've covered this in Part 1 - 'The Bitch, Premating Prep,' as it can also be given to bitches.

These free radicals can damage cells, so ensuring a plentiful supply of vitamin E to scavenge and protect.

Co-enzyme Q10 is another supplement that is an antioxidant. It protects cells from damage and plays an integral part in the metabolism; it has been studied for its benefits on low sperm counts and poor motility.

Lastly, Zinc is a supplement that could significantly increase the total semen collection volume, sperm motility and the percentage of normal sperm - increasing the overall male's reproductive function. Zinc in humans plays an essential role in spermatogenesis, sperm formation in the testis, and the repair of damaged DNA.

Other sperm aiding products may also include vitamin C, L-carnitine, L-arginine, glutathione, selenium, folic acid, carotenoids, N-acetylcysteine and omega-9.

Stud Service Withdrawal

There may become a point when you decide to restrict or withdraw your dog from public stud, and there are many reasons why this may be the case.

- **Hard work & Time Consuming** - Managing stud enquiries can be time consuming, you'll have all levels of bitch owners approach you for your dog's services, and many may be demanding and mentally exhausting. You'll also have parties express a lot of interest and then fail to keep to their commitment, changing their mind last minute, finding more suitable studs for their choices and priorities.

Breeding tends to be 'last minute', I always advise bitch owners to do their research well in advance and notify the stud owner on day 1 of the season. You will have people contacting you to use your stud 'today'. Some stud owners can feel offended by this lack of preparation, and so politely decline, others will believe flexibility is one of the key services that should be offered.

Some stud owners have attempted to manage these predicaments with limited 'lock-ins', meaning a bitch owner needs to put a deposit down in advance to secure the stud dog at a set stud fee.

- **Behavioural changes** - Behavioural changes can be breed and dog dependent. The dynamics can change in your own household when one of your dogs becomes a regular stud. You'll need to manage any conflict that may arise with other dogs they experience. This is one reason why AI is preferred by many, as it removes a lot of the dominance association; however, this practice does not guarantee there won't be any behavioural changes.

- **Canine illness** - If your dog is unwell, has underlying issues causing hormone imbalances, requires any treatment or medication. You must check with your vet about what impact this may have on his fertility. Heat exposure can also have a negative effect, whether that be a raised temperature with illness or even hydro pools or sunbathing. Regular semen testing will help identify these potential problems early.

- **Low fertility** - Fertility will decline with age, and a stud dog should be checked regularly from 7 years old. A male may just have substandard fertility at any age identified during a fertility assessment. It's then your decision to remove the dog from public stud, or share the relevant information with the bitch owners to make an informed decision. It's not fair to withhold this information and breed with little hope of success.

- **Unable to perform -** If a male's libido decreases, they should be taken to the vet and checked for any illness or injury preventing them from performing. Age may also affect libido (either being too young and immature, or elderly).

- **Too popular** - Some stud owners may decide to control the demand of their stud by, at times, limiting his availability. This stops the gene pool for the breed from being flooded and helps keep demand for the stud when only siring quality puppies. It's hard to actively manage this level of interest and demand strategically, but if the male is desired to a level that this sort of management is required, then it's certainly possible.

- **No longer popular** - It may be the case a new health test for the breed becomes available, and the offered stud dog is affected or a carrier of the condition. Or it may become apparent the sire is producing puppies with a consistent issue even to different females, so the demand for his services declines.

High stud fees may price you out of the market, or difficult geographical locations may also negatively impact a stud demand. Other reasons include younger males new to the arena, with particular highly desired assets or traits.

Stud Demand - supply & demand

When you own a stud dog, you'll realise that matings are like buses, you'll have nothing for months and then more than enough bitches within a few weeks. This is because many bitches are triggered by seasonal weather changes, which can then cause one female to bring in all the other females she lives with, causing them to cycle together.

With this in mind, you should effectively manage your stud's matings. All bitch owners should receive the same consistent service. It's not fair to allow one female owner to have three matings over a long period because they can't be bothered to ovulation test. Then another female who has tested to be given his fourth mating of that week. Proactive bitch owers should be considered a priority because they have invested in detecting ovulation.

Your stud contract should be clear about how many matings you'll cover and what circumstances. I have known some owners only offer one mating and will only accept bitches who have been ovulation tested, this isn't typical, but it does demonstrate the efforts the stud owner is willing to go to ensure all bitches receive the stud's 'best'.

How many matings is too many?

Crufts is like Mecca for many of my peers. It's always been a pretty lucky dog show for me, and even when not showing, I still like to go and support my breed. A good friend, Margriet, has flown over from Holland for the last few years, and we make a long weekend of it all. Coincidentally we only met because I used her stud dog called Jagger. I drove over and collected chilled semen after stumbling across him on Facebook, and we've been good friends ever since.

This particular year, we met up with friends at a Persian restaurant the night before driving to Crufts. I'm not sure how it came about, but the joke ended up being on me, as the group convinced the restaurateur that it was my birthday, and I was unknowingly delivered a serving of birthday cake with a sparkler and joyful singing. I just went along with it.

We then headed up to Crufts the following day, met up with more friends, and ended up in TGI Fridays for drinks and food, and yes, the same happened again. If you've never experienced a TGI Friday birthday song, then wow, you should. This time I received a cake and a balloon crown. I was less impressed but again took it for the team and carried on. Aren't my friends funny?

The following day we attended the show, and I had booked Best in Show tickets, as I had only ever watched it on the TV. We decided to have Nandos before the event. We sat at the table for 2, and the birthday song started within minutes. I glared at my Dutch friend Margriet, but they walked passed me to the table behind, Phew.

I was sick to the back of my teeth of Birthday celebrations when it wasn't even my birthday. It was way too much of a good thing. So how much is too much of a good thing for stud dogs covering multiple bitches in a day?

A frequently used healthy stud dog could cover two bitches in one day with no drama. I had this situation with my own dogs and bred my male to two bitches with a 12 hour gap, both ovulation tested and both confirmed in pup.

However, this should not be a regular occurrence. Sperm production will be supply and demand. The more used, the more the body will produce to meet demand. When a male is 'over used', he will be forced to use sperm that is not mature. Immature semen will have a much higher abnormality rate, and it will not be correctly formed and, therefore, will not be able to fertilise an egg. As a result, bitches will miss or carry much smaller litters.

Depending on what's stipulated in your contract, a small litter may mean they are still entitled to a remate. Missed bitches are always a disappointment for everyone and will do nothing but impact your future calendar with remate commitments.

As the stud owner, it's your interest to protect your stud dog and his future fertility. Over-using a young male could do long term damage to sperm production, hence why it's recommended that males are not used until 12 months old.

Chemical Castrations

It's strange to talk about castration in a breeding book, but I thought it worth mentioning as many people aren't aware of the available options.

You may be considering castrating your stud dog, which will write off his ability to produce any progeny in the future. There is an option to chemically castrate your dog using products like Superlorin or Tardak. They are simple implants put under the skin and can be removed or worn off after 6 or 12 months. I'll be honest, there's very little research on how fertile a male is after the removal or 'wear-off' of the implant because if the male became sterile, there's no way of knowing if that would have happened regardless of the implant.

It is an option to consider if you want to possibly use a male in the future. The dog should be semen checked 3 months after the removal or 'wearing-off'. If the sample quality is poor, 'stud supplements' should be given and rechecked in another 3 months. If the semen is still poor, this will most likely not change. I have seen cases of males making a full fertility recovery after the implant and others that have not.

An additional option would be to collect from the male before he's chemically castrated, and this collection to be frozen for future use. A small number of veterinary reproduction specialists across the U.K will be able to do this for you, as it's not a standard service offered by local veterinary practices.

Future Breeding Opportunities

Frozen Semen

The future is unknown to us, and you never know when your dog's reproductive function will stop. It may be sudden and unexpected with an illness or, even worse, death. If your dog has been diagnosed with a terminal illness, it may be possible to collect and freeze some of this semen.

There are reproduction specialists around the country that will be able to process and store the semen in liquid nitrogen. This has the capability of the semen being stored with no time limits. This option allows you to consider the impact on your bloodline, the breed and its future without time restrictions.

This opportunity should be harnessed by breeders because the possible potential it may give you in the future is almost limitless. Stored semen could generate future income opportunities if sold to interested breeders. These semen collections can even be DNA profiled for conditions that weren't knowingly in existence when the dog was alive. This information within the genetic material could help re-establish a breed.

Another benefit to frozen semen is it can be shipped internationally. If you plan to import semen, this should be done well in advance of the semen being needed. Depending on the country, there can be various customs and clearance procedures that can delay the shipment.

Save & Store

It's recommended that semen collections are taken whilst the dog is in his prime. The better the semen concentration, the more breeding dosages a single collection will give you for future use. Under particular or extreme circumstances, if the semen is of poor quality, it's still worth having a specialist look at the viability.

The breeding dosages are typically stored in 0.5ml 'straws' or 'pellets' with a concentration of 150 million sperm per ml. This typically means two straws (or a set number of pellets) are a breeding dose. This is the requirement for insemination, provided the post-thaw evaluation is good (the semen is thawed after processing to check viability). Because the semen has been frozen, it's more fragile and less robust, so it needs to be done by trans-cervical insemination (TCI). During the TCI, the semen is deposited through the cervix to give it the best possible chance of fertilising the eggs rather than a standard dog-to-dog AI, which is trans-vaginal. A TCI can again, only be provided by a handful of veterinary reproductive specialists in the UK, unlike standard trans-vaginal AI's, which just require a trained individual.

The collection, processing and storage of the semen is moderately priced, given the future capability it gives you. The expense typically arises when the semen is to be used. Rigorous Progesterone ovulation testing is required to identify the optimal window for the TCI. Insemination is carried out three days post-ovulation or five days after the LH surge.

Chapter 10 - Stud contracts summary

During this chapter, we have covered:

- The relevance and protection a stud contract provides and the information that should be included.
- The importance of correctly maintaining and managing a successful stud dog.
- The benefits of using additional breeding options to increase your stud's breeding longevity.

Part 2 - The Stud Summary

There can be a lot of responsibility and pressure to provide a service that is reliable and fit for purpose when offering a dog at stud. You'll need to decide if you plan to handle your own dog or use a professional service offered by a skilled expert, and if so, ensure they're competent and reliable.

You should lead by example by health testing your dog and encouraging and educating bitch owners to do the same. This will help deflect any negative experiences or the stud being unfairly blamed or tarred for producing puppies with health conditions. If you identify a consistent health issue with puppies across numerous litters, you should reassess the suitability of offering your male at public stud.

You are the gatekeeper of how the breed develops in the future, so patience and high standards are critical for a stud to benefit the breed and its longevity.

Want more help?

Owning a stud dog can feel isolating. You are most likely dealing with all different types of people regularly. It's hard when you don't have dog-minded friends to sense check some circumstances or situations.

This book is just the introduction to skillfully managing a stud dog, it's not possible to cover every situation or eventuality that may occur. For this reason, I've decided to build a community called the Home Breeder Hub, where like-minded productive stud owners can share current issues or difficulties they may be experiencing. Do you:

- Lack the confidence to deal with bitch owners effectively?
- Feel an unrealistic pressure to ensure all females that use your male conceive?
- Doubt your dog's fertility? Or suitability to be at public stud?

- Wonder if you could better support your bitch owners by offering stud packages?

Then the Home Breeder Hub may be for you.

Even if you own only male dogs and have never bred a litter yourself, you will still be expected to support your bitch owners. In the Hub, I'm available to support and advise you and your dogs. We can tackle any complex challenges together and share your successes with pride. It can feel daunting and confusing when you offer paid stud services with only a few trusted peers around you for support.

Home Breeder Hub - Very Important Breeder (ViB) Access

The Home Breeder Hub is a paid monthly membership for the conscientious dog owners, who I like to call ViB's, Very Important Breeders. This is a fabulous community of breeders who want to raise the bar and seek reliable, supportive advice. The Hub is the only way you'll have direct access to me, so I can support you on your breeding journey and experiences. If you are dedicated to investing in this pastime, then the Hub is the place for you.

What do you get as a ViB?

- Fortnightly online breeding support sessions offering an opportunity for you to discuss your dog's specific breeding needs and issues - ***Value £197***
- Monthly breeding educational webinars including guest speakers - ***Value £97***
- Quarterly printed and posted publication straight to your letterbox - ***Value £97***
- Unlimited access to all resources within the Hub - ***Priceless!***
- Access to the community forum for more in-depth doggy discussions - ***Value £97***

Book reader offer for you

You can register for the Home Breeder Hub and claim your first month for just **£9.99** by going to **www.caninefamilyplanner.com/DSVIB**

- PART THREE: The Mating -

CHAPTER 11

The Mating

Many moons ago, when I worked as a Learning & Development Consultant, I trained people or found someone that could. I was based near Hayward's Heath in Sussex and commuted to 'the London' office every two weeks. I had a desk next to my team colleagues, and we'd catch up on various work-related tasks.

In passing, one team member, Ellie, mentioned she had twins and held an officer's position for some sort of Twin Birth association. They hold various annual events and social gatherings to support the parents.

I found it all very intriguing as I recalled one of my childhood best friends saying that when she had children, she would have twins because they 'run in her family'.

I'm sure it was something like every second daughter on the male side of the family had them. True to form her first pregnancy, she had two twin boys. I also recall a set of identical twins at secondary school, but you could always tell them apart as one was way trendier than the other.

My colleague Ellie explained her twins were the result of fertility treatment. 'In vitro fertilisation' or IVF as we know it, the egg and sperm are combined in-vitro, meaning it was performed outside the living organism/body in a laboratory.

With this in mind, I was still surprised to find out such associations existed. I guess you don't know, what you don't know. There's been around a 75% increase in twins over the last 30 years due to the impact of fertility treatments.

This situation had never been on my radar because it never needed to be. Which is a bit like dog breeding and matings for some.

Ignorance is bliss, and most people think you can just let two dogs have a run around the garden; they start flirting, and in minutes the deed is done. After a twenty-minute tie, you go home, and in nine weeks, she'll pop out a litter of eight.

I can tell you that occurrence is rare, like rocking horse poo.

In the past, you would pay for a stud dog that came hand-in-hand with an equally experienced owner/stud handler, who would ensure (90% of the time) you received a good mating for the fee you paid. This kind of job isn't for everyone. This meant the stud gene pool was much smaller than today. These dogs were highly regarded and popular, as people had confidence in them and their ability to get a mating and sire quality pups.

But like with IVF for humans, there have been developments to make the 'conception' process much more manageable. Not only for the dogs involved but for the owners too. This has ultimately led to the increasing gene pool of stud dogs because it's no longer required for the stud dog's owner to be a handling expert. A litter can result in newer mating methods without the dog and bitch having ever met.

We don't IVF with dogs, but we do AI, artificially inseminate, similar to IUI (Intrauterine Insemination)in humans. A doctor inserts the sperm directly into a woman's cervix (or fallopian tubes or uterus).

The increased popularity of AI means there have never been as many dogs available in the public stud arena as there are now. The possibilities are endless. That paired with the accessibility of reproduction services offered outside of the traditional veterinary landscape and the flexibility of shipping semen around the world, stud choices are no longer limited by geographical location.

When to Mate: Ovulation Confirmed

When ovulation has been confirmed by your chosen method, you should also be advised when to mate. Typically 48 hours post-ovulation, it could be immediately because the eggs have already matured. The bitch owner needs to determine how many matings are recommended and at what schedule.

Typically with Cytology, I always recommend two matings 48 hours apart. If they have progesterone ovulation tested, then one mating at the optimal time is more than sufficient. Many bitch owners still like to have two matings, as traditionally offered as a stud service. If this is the case, breed 48 hours apart (four and six days after the LH surge). The LH surge is connected to egg release, which means eggs will be ready for fertilisation four days after the surge.

Most stud owners are incredibly flexible when fitting in matings, especially when the bitch owner has ovulation tested and knows the correct timing. I have driven 200 miles to a stud for a 7am breeding and have also mated my own dogs at 6am before heading to a day of dog show judging. When you are working in a restricted window of time, needs must.

I've had clients progesterone ovulation test as late as 11pm, then be advised to mate immediately. I then received a text message to say the bitch wasn't overly willing for a 3am mating. I'm sure she wasn't! I suggest to anyone with the progesterone result of 'mate immediately', so late in the day or plans to drive to another country for the stud, at least do it on a good night's sleep.

If you are not carrying out a dog-to-dog (both present) mating but instead having chilled semen shipped, then it's key the bitch owners are proactive with ovulation testing. Most packages will need to be issued Monday to Thursday before the last post for effective and timely shipping, as weekends and bank holidays will add delays.

Natural Mating

Both dog owners should discuss the options for the impending mating in advance. Regardless of the method of mating, the stud dog should be comfortable in the surroundings. Preferably both dogs should urinate in advance and have not recently eaten before the mating.

Natural

Natural matings should only ever be conducted with an experienced handler. Not all stud owners are able, or wish to handle their own dogs, so they may require a third party to be drafted in to assist. Assistance is necessary for both the safety of the dog and bitch. You may be able to find a suitable stud handler through personal or veterinary recommendations or online research.

Every dog has their own personality and quirks. The stud handler will know what methods will give the stud confidence to perform, but also with the least possible stress to the bitch.

They should be able to control the situation, notice if the bitch is too short or tall, and then problem solve quickly to fix these issues - such as using a stack of mats, steps or a slope to adjust heights. The owner's absence may also improve a stud dog's confidence and libido, but there will be many more issues and resolutions gained with experience.

Bitches can react in as many ways as you can imagine when it comes to a mating. Some are super flirty and happy to be mounted, others think it is the most horrifying thing in the world, and typically you won't find this out until you attempt to get the dogs bred, especially maiden bitches. Acknowledgement should also be taken that the dogs may be in their second socialisation fear phase, connected to sexual maturity. If the experience is not managed, it could negatively impact both dogs.

It's a time sensitive issue to ensure she's covered during her optimal fertile window.

Maiden Mating

Maiden dogs are those that are not proven. This means the male has not sired any puppies, or the female has not birthed any puppies. Maiden matings, due to inexperience, can result in a mixed bag of opportunities and challenges.

Once comfortable, some dogs successfully achieve a mating after a matter of time; others may be clueless instead of looking like they are confidently achieving the 64 arts of the Kamasutra. They actually are achieving nothing but exhaustion, even with 100% effort. In this instance, the stud handler would need to guide and assist him in penetrating whilst supporting and correctly positioning the female. For this reason, it's beneficial for stud owners to physically touch and handle their dog regularly, so the dog is used to close contact, especially around his genitalia.

If you plan to breed your own dogs (male and female), who are most likely maiden, be aware of the natural dynamics of dogs living together. Typically the female is the dominant of the group. It can sometimes be difficult for these roles to be forgotten to allow the male to confidently 'perform' when needed. Discouraging a male for casually mounting a bitch can harm his future willingness, so you need the foresight not to do this if you plan to use your own male. It would be better to keep them physically separated than to tell him off for mounting at the incorrect time when she is in season. Issues such as this can lead us to seek alternative options.

To tie, or not to tie, that is the question?

When breeding naturally, it's deemed the pinnacle of success when the dogs tie. Many have witnessed this whilst on holiday abroad, most probably from your balcony or when walking to the beach, you'll see two dogs back-to-back looking out for each other.

This happens when the bulbus glands of the male swell inside the bitch, causing them to 'lock' together. For this reason, I always call them the locking nuts. You'll see many novice pet owner groups asking why their male has two sets of testicles, of which they don't. As we all know, one set is the testes, and the 'other bumps' in the groin area are the dog's bulbus glandis. They can become rather large and hard when a male is excited, regardless of a bitch being present, causing them to 'knot' even when not tied.

During a mating, the glands expand and 'knot' to stop the male from withdrawing. The female is generally stimulated by them and tends to clench onto them. This is a tie and can typically last up to 30 minutes. It was deemed in yesteryear, that the longer the tie, the better the mating, but this isn't the case. During the tie, the male uses the opportunity to push the semen up to the female's cervix with his prostate fluid. You'll see this prostatic fluid when the tie ends and they part.

However, a tie is not needed for a successful breeding.

As long as the male has ejaculated in the female, you may see the male's little rear foot dance once all the thrusting has stopped while mounted. His anus and base of his tail should then start twitching, which indicates ejaculation.

I've confirmed many bitches in pup with a 'slip' mating; this is when the male hasn't tied, but has ejaculated. There are many reasons a male may not be able to tie - height and size differences, the female doesn't respond to his bulbus glands, is not in the optimum window, or may have vaginal obstructions. Such internal obstructions blocking the vaginal canal can result in a more difficult mating, and a tie is more difficult.

This is when artificial insemination is a great option to be considered, to help avoid uncomfortable or stressful mating, and ensure semen is deposited as near to the cervix as possible.

Physical Female Checks

The female should always be physically checked internally by the stud handler before any breedings, natural or AI, to identify if any obstructions may make the breeding more difficult or complex.

Vaginal Prolapse (Hyperplasia)

This condition is seen more commonly in brachycephalic (flat-faced) breeds, including French Bulldogs, Boxers, Bulldogs and Mastiff types. The condition is due to the excessive swelling of the vaginal wall typically triggered by Oestrogen hormone during the early stages of a season. The swelling causes an internal, fleshy mass to protrude past the vulva opening. The condition tends to reoccur every season once it's presented. There is no direct negative impact on fertility, but the mass can cause an obstruction making a natural mating difficult.

For this reason, AI is an easier option allowing the semen to be deposited past the mass. The protruding mass will recede and return to normal as the female changes through her fertility cycle. It's unknown if the condition is hereditary.

It's advised to keep the protruding tissue clean, free from dirt, and moist, to prevent bacteria from travelling up the vaginal tract. Season knickers may be a consideration or a natural antibacterial spray like Colloidal Silver.

Vaginal Strictures & Polyps

Vestibulo-vaginal strictures are a collective term used for any defect which leads to the narrowing or any form of vaginal obstruction. These restrict the introduction of a penis, making penetration by a male painful. Many of these females will object to a natural breeding.

AI is the perfect solution to this problem, and bizarrely many bitches with these issues will whelp normally, most probably due to the influence of hormones.

The most common obstructions I experience can be felt in the lower vaginal canal with a gloved finger.

I consider Vaginal Polyps to be small surface tissue lumps that result in stenosis, the narrowing of the vagina. These can easily be manipulated and worked around with an AI tube.

I refer to strictures as all other forms of obstructions such as 'dorsoventral bands' and 'vaginal septae'. The first are thick, strong bands that stretch from the top to the bottom of the vaginal canal, the latter are bands of tissue that divide the vagina into two parts - making pockets. The decision when inseminating is, do you go to the left or right? From my experience, I've found the side easier to access seems to be the right choice.

Some abnormalities are more prolific in certain breeds, so heritability cannot be excluded.

Chapter 11 - The mating summary

During this chapter, we have covered:

- The enhanced benefits of using a qualified and trained expert to assist and safely support the physical mating of two dogs.
- The differences between natural and artificial insemination breeding methods.
- The importance of pre-mating checks to ensure the best chances of a stress-free mating.

CHAPTER 12
Artificial Insemination

Why Artificially Inseminate?

There are many reasons why some owners (dog or bitch) may prefer Artificial Insemination (AI) as the mating method. AI can be an ideal way to introduce less confident males to matings, by firstly experiencing the physical changes and reactions when aroused in a safe 'non-threatening' environment. Then for him to later mate naturally with established confidence.

AI is a perfect way of overcoming many problems a natural breeding may present, including:

- A significant size difference between the dogs
- An injured stud that's unable to mount
- Extreme "temporary" temperament changes, submissive or dominant bitch or dog
- Inexperienced stud

Even if the dogs could breed naturally, some owners still prefer this method because they feel insemination has many more additional benefits:

- Semen can be quality checked before insemination to reduce stud liability
- Less stressful for the dogs
- Reduced negative breeding behaviours - disassociation/no mounting/leg cocking
- Faster - no lengthy and unnecessary ties
- Safely control a dog's experience within their second fear phase

- Can meet in a neutral location - such as the fertility clinic rather than within the home, providing flexibility of meeting point and personal safety.

General AI Practice

Artificial insemination is collecting semen from a dog and then artificially inseminating it into a female. There are three different types of AI, but for now, we'll concentrate on the most common, intra-vaginal, which can be conducted by an experienced handler who is competent but not necessarily a vet.

Collecting the semen from the male is not overly comparable to humans, though that method will most probably work! It requires a competent person to stimulate the bulbus glandis, which typically happens during mating and causes the tie. This will encourage a natural response from the dog, leading to the production of semen.

The ejaculation actually occurs in three parts. The first fraction removes any debris from his penile urethra tract, and in most instances usually ends up on the floor.

The second fraction is the semen rich fraction and is the section that needs to be collected. It's typically a small quantity of around 0.5 - 2ml, and white in colour. Then finally, the third fraction is 'the wash', this is a prostatic fluid that pushes the semen up the vaginal canal during the tie, so the total quantity can be considerable. If the male were to naturally mate, the third fraction that you would see leak out when they separate.

When it comes to AI methods, the whole purpose is to collect the second fraction with a small amount of the third fraction to create a favourable environment for the semen and a suitable amount of fluid to be flushed through the AI tube into the female.

Is the more collected the better with AI?

People boast about 20ml plus collections when, in fact, all they have done is dilute down their collection and once inseminated, there's more chance of the fluid leaking or seeping back out of the vagina. This quantity is only helpful if a large 'over collection' is required to collect as much sperm as possible, most likely due to a poor Total Sperm Count. This fluid volume can then be processed by spinning using a centrifuge that forces the semen to the bottom of the receptacle, forming a pellet. This pellet can then be reconstituted into a smaller fluid volume, resulting in a higher total sperm concentration. The collection must be treated with care throughout this process, so it's not irreparably damaged. This level of processing is not commonplace; hence such large quantity collections are usually not beneficial.

'Total inseminated volume' amounts are typically between 2 and 8ml depending on the breed, the stud and how often he's used. The more inseminated, the more diluted the sample will become, and there is more risk of 'overfill' resulting in excess fluid being expelled.

How successful is AI?

Trans-vaginal AI is no more or less successful than a natural mating if the female hasn't been ovulation tested. It doesn't matter how the semen 'arrives' if the eggs aren't mature for fertilisation, this is why ovulation testing is key.

The experience is significantly less stressful for all involved and may be quicker. If ovulation has been detected through testing, AI generally increases the chances of conception as less of the sample is 'lost' in transition, making it more efficient.

From my experience, there seems to be a small percentage of the working breeds that are less likely to conceive from AI. I feel it's because they are more highly attuned and are fully aware they haven't had a mating, so why would they be pregnant? I've found these unusual girls benefit from a lot of play, flirting with the males before the AI, and for her to be mounted for the collection.

An added bonus for these females would be for her to have a natural breeding after her AI, if physically possible. I know some breeders are keen on this protocol. I suggest that the AI is first to ensure the optimal time is covered, and then the natural mating is attempted later with little pressure and minimal stress, merely as a 'top up'.

Does AI mean fewer matings needed?

The success of an AI really does depend on the ovulation timing of the female. She needs to be inseminated at the most fertile time. This means she should have been progesterone ovulation tested to identify when the eggs are mature for fertilisation (the oestrus phase of her cycle).

If you've ovulation tested the female and the optimal time for mating has been identified, you only need one mating to occur, whether naturally or by AI. If you have made no attempt to identify her fertile window, it's recommended, regardless of the method, to mate, miss a day and mate a second time, 48 hours apart. This method gives the largest window of possible conception - as the semen should be viable up to 2-3 days after the last mating, so 6 days after the first.

Are AI litters bigger?

Technically, no. It really doesn't matter how the semen gets to the cervix (the opening of the uterus), it comes down to if the timing of the mating is right. From my experience, I would say AI litters are marginally larger. I feel that this is probably because less fluid is lost during the mating itself and the fact that it's actually deposited deeper into the reproductive tract than during a natural mating, enabling more semen to reach the cervix.

AI matings tend to be quicker than a natural mating because there is no physical tie with this method. The person with AI experience should stimulate the female, if possible, after depositing the semen to imitate a natural mating. This physical re-enactment is good for her body and psychologically, so she's aware that a mating has taken place and her body reacts accordingly.

Is AI allowed for registered dogs?

The Kennel Club will accept any litters produced by intra-vaginal AI from a dog in the UK or overseas, but they require an additional form to be completed. You'll need to check with other alternative registries if that is also the case.

Litters produced from the mating pair will be accepted, but their offspring should be able to produce a litter naturally before they are involved in AI. If the parents produce subsequent litters naturally, then this restriction placed by the Kennel Club is lifted.

I must highlight the Kennel Club will only know any of this information due to your willingness to share it on their requested form.

Other forms of AI

Surgical AI is another technique that a vet should only conduct as sedation is required. This is typically used when frozen semen is deposited directly into the uterus for the best success rate. This method can also allow for a visual inspection of the reproductive organs and any observations that may highlight possible fertility issues.

This practice has been banned in the U.K since February 2019 because it's felt this extreme measure to achieve pregnancy raises more significant ethical issues - regarding a female's natural ability to reproduce without severe medical intervention.

Trans-cervical insemination (TCI) should only be conducted by a vet, who would use an endoscope - a tube with a light and camera attached. It's used so frozen semen can be deposited through the cervix or, in exceptional cases, for females with a history of difficult conception. The female is not sedated, and a trained hand is required to find the cervix opening.

Additional Flexibility

Male collections can be split to cover more than one mating or one bitch. This provides more flexibility for potential mating clashes or to help cover her entire optimal fertility window.

The male collection can be chilled and shipped worldwide. Most semen extenders last between 3 to 8 days with a constant temperature source. A trained person will be required to reheat, analyse and inseminate the semen when necessary. Typically this is achieved by warming the collection in a water-bath at 37°C for around 15 minutes. The progress can be checked under the microscope and warmed for longer, or add a performance extender if needed. Once the sperm is active and motile, it can then be inseminated into the bitch in the same way any standard trans-vaginal insemination would be carried out.

The chilled semen option, if processed correctly by all parties and used within the time frame available, can be as good as a dog-to-dog AI with the required ovulation testing. Costs associated with this option are reasonable and sometimes even more cost-effective if there was a significant distance between the dogs that would have otherwise been travelled.

AI Husbandry

The mating pair should remain separated until the point the AI is required. Allowing the couple together beforehand can result in the male becoming stressed, his collection being unnecessarily lost or general upset and frustration between the mating pair. The separation ensures the stud remains keen, is easier to collect from and typically produces a better sample.

There is some basic housekeeping required for AI and handling semen. My preference is for all equipment to be single-use, clean and sterile. Gloves should have no latex, nor should the syringes. The AI tube length will depend on the breed and length of the dog.

There are a variety of tubes that can be used; some are flexible, others rigid. My choice typically depends on the breed and possible vaginal obstructions. In their presence, I will always start with rigid. I typically aim to AI no less than 6 inches and up to 12 inches deep. I will mark the AI tube with 6,9 and 12 inches measures for a small number of breeds. This helps me ensure I push past all obstructions and deposit the semen as close to the cervix as possible.

Inserting the AI tube should follow the natural angle of the vulva, typically around 45°. Once resistance is felt, the tube should be straightened horizontally to 180° and then slowly pushed further with a gentle 'screwing' action. If needed, apply some pressure to push past the pseudo-cervix.

Semen is pretty robust, but any temperature shocks should be avoided. The room temperature should be mild, and any equipment, storage units or heat plates should be kept around 37°C. This means the person carrying out the AI may make minor alterations to their practices in the winter compared to the summer if the environment temperature fluctuates.

I like to use a collection funnel that feeds directly into a syringe, meaning that no semen is lost in the transition from the collection vessel to a syringe for the AI. Many use a sandwich bag as they are readily available, robust, hard to rip, malleable and transparent to see the transition from 2nd to 3rd fraction. A clear bag also helps identify contaminants like urine or blood. The issue with such bags is that they offer little protection from temperature shock.

I've known people to use collection cups and beakers of various forms. If this is your collection preference, I would recommend a Styrofoam cup due to its insulation properties and single-use for hygiene. I also worry about cups because the collection can be easily and quickly lost if they are dropped.

A hot tip, if you carry out your own AI and manage to go into the bladder, which is easy to do, you'll see that the AI tube will fill up with urine. Don't worry. Leave that tube in place and insert a second AI tube - you'll be unlikely to hit the bladder again as the opening will already be filled with the first tube.

Another good tip is that if you are inseminating a female with vaginal strictures, resulting in poor seasonal drainage, it may be worth inserting an AI tube to draw off any excess bloody discharge that may be trapped. Discard this tube and use a second tube for the semen insemination, as the blood is toxic to semen.

If the blood you draw off is excessive, over 10ml, and smells foul, I would most certainly speak to a vet for a course of antibiotics. I would also recommend females with such symptoms are drawn off daily throughout their season to prevent any build-up, so the bitch owner will need to identify and manage this issue before breeding.

Though extremely rare, some females suffer vaginal haemorrhaging during a season. The blood is excessive, with up to 100ml of blood a day leaving large pools on the ground. It's believed to be due to excessively high oestrogen levels. Treatment would include vaginal drainage, flushing, AI and antibiotic treatment. However, fertility in these females is poor, and spaying is advised.

Lucky me, I've had a female who I had bred with this issue; on her first season, she developed Pyometra, we treated it with Alizin and Antibiotics rather than a spay, and on the following season, we were advised to breed her. I drew off over 80ml of blood per day, and gave a course of antibiotics. She did not conceive, so I decided to have her spayed. The blood was so excessive that I put her in seasonal pants to help control the leakage. She was from a litter of four, one of three girls and to my knowledge, she was the only female to have this issue in the litter. She was a granddaughter/father mating with a high COI of 21.1%, which makes you wonder if that was something to do with it. It's proven the higher the COI, the smaller the litter sizes.

Tipping

In my opinion, 'Tipping' the female by raising her rear legs after AI is not essential if the AI is deep enough into the body. People like to do this to improve conception rates. I've even heard of vets balancing a 60kg Great Dane's rear legs on their shoulders! Instead, I prefer to always imitate a tie by stimulating the bitch with a gloved finger and feathering the vaginal wall to trigger the female to contract and draw the semen in.

Once the female has been inseminated, it's advisable that she is kept calm and quiet, possibly crated, for an hour and that she does not urinate during this time. It is also a myth that she'll urinate the semen out, but the urine can alter the pH level of the tract, which may have a negative effect.

Semen Quality Control

One of the many benefits of AI is assessing the semen before inseminating the female. This can be done at both macro-level, assessing the amount and colour and at a micro-level under a microscope.

A trained person will be able to confirm the concentration, movement (motility) and development/shape (morphology) of the semen, advising on the overall quality and how that may impact the chances of breeding success.

A good semen collection can vary from 150 million to 2 billion, with 70-80% motility and 80% normal morphology.

The total sperm count is the collected volume multiplied by the million per ml. Most clinics will use a photometer to work out the million per ml. Working this out by eye using a microscope and counting chamber (with some mathematics) is an acquired skill that can be extremely time-consuming.

I host a 'One Billion + Stud Club' for my client's dogs. You'll notice no toy breeds are listed because the total volume collected is typically relevant to the dog's size, affecting the total sperm count. It currently stands at (table overleaf):

One Billion + Stud Club League Table				
Ranking	**Concentration (Billion)**	**Volume (ml)**	**Breed**	**Name**
1	1.50	10.5	German Shepherd Dog	Rocky
2	1.28	7.5	German Shepherd Dog	Zeus
3	1.17	9.0	XL American Bully	Smokey
4	1.07	6.0	English Bulldog	Mr Biggs
5	1.06	7.5	English Bulldog	Lewis
6	1.05	6.0	English Bulldog	Mr Northwest

The minimum concentration collection for AI should be no less than 100 million. If this is the case, then other methods of AI, like TCI, may be needed to help improve the chances of success. Knowing the total sperm count is also beneficial if the semen is split, processed for chilling or identified as a substandard collection that can be improved with enhancers.

Dual Sires

Most registries will accept dual sired litters. This is when a bitch conceives puppies from two individual males. I've heard of many accidental matings that have resulted in split litters of puppies, but there are times when you may want to intentionally do this.

A dual sired litter, if successful, means you'll increase the breed's gene pool quicker which is a significant advantage for rare breeds or numerically small populated breeds. It's also a good option for ageing bitches or females where you have limited breeding opportunities.

Registries will require the DNA testing of both sires and the dam. Along with all puppies in the litter, each puppy's heritage will need to be identified.

Breeders opting for TCI of frozen semen have been known to also cover the bitch with fresh semen from a different sire. This practice will increase the chances of "some puppies" rather than her not conceiving. The frozen semen has a lower success rate by virtue and possibly missing the entire breeding opportunity.

When discussing planned dual sired litters, I'm referring to intra-vaginal insemination. Both males are collected, and the bitch is inseminated. This option may be less attractive if you have two stud fees to pay, as the chances of achieving a dual sired litter are pretty low, even when intentional, and all the puppies will still need to be DNA tested. Not to mention the logistics of having three dogs present simultaneously.

It's certainly an option for some owners in some particular situations, but the science of achieving a 50/50 litter has not yet been defined. Many variables such as semen concentration, progressive motility, abnormality rates, and internal pH differences between the two males and the female must be managed to ensure success.

Breeding Protocol

Waiting for a female to come into season can feel like being a kid again at Christmas. It can feel like it's taking FOR-EV-ER...

But they do like to surprise us. Fast weather and temperature change can trigger bitches, causing them to come into heat early or delay it. Daily observations of her behaviour and physical changes will help build patterns.

It's good to have a clearly defined process for when the bitch does come into season to avoid anyone making rushed and possibly bad choices in a panic. The plan should be implemented when day one of her season is recognised.

Day one would be the first-day vaginal blood is observed. This may not necessarily be on the floor, particularly in long-coated breeds. A cotton bud can be gently inserted into the bottom of the vulva to check. Doing this daily will help identify day one of the season. It's also good to have white or light coloured bedding to observe any possible discharge.

When day one of the season is identified, she is in the Proestrus phase. Start any supplements such as Folic Acid (see Part 1 - Premating Prep), and if you haven't wormed in advance, do it no later than now. Contact the stud dog owner so they can pencil it in their calendar and identify any potential issues with mating clashes or availability.

You'll also need to organise ovulation testing to get booked between days 6 - 9 of the season for Progesterone testing. Retesting will be every four days maximum, so look how this might be impacted by weekends and bank holidays. If cytology is the chosen method, start day 6 of the season and look at the retesting schedule every 3 days, unless advised otherwise.

I recommend progesterone ovulation testing earlier in the day, if possible and better still, before eating breakfast or lunch. The results will be processed by the afternoon, allowing for the same day mating if needed. Hormone levels are highest in the morning and can dip a little during the day due to the body's metabolism, which is why, typically, a standard deviation of around 20% is acceptable. It's preferred that the bloods for each retest are taken roughly at the same time of day and are fasted bloods. If you are disciplined with your ovulation testing, you shouldn't experience unexpected surprises. Therefore, will have the time to plan your trip to the stud without any considerable inconvenience.

Stud Packages

Many stud owners offer 'stud packages'. They will ovulation test, provide the stud service, and ultrasound scan the bitch to confirm her pregnancy status. Whilst I totally understand the benefit of only dealing with one party, making the planning and logistics seamless, from my experience, the service may not always be as professional as you may expect. Ovulation results and mating dates may be manipulated to fit into an existing scheduled diary.

Bitch owners can sometimes be left with false hope after the stud owner has confirmed pregnancy (as they can feel under pressure to do so). For the female to be later rescanned by someone different after showing little physical change, only for the bitch not to be pregnant after all - to be given excuses such as total litter absorption by the stud owner - which, from my experience, is extremely rare.

I know this is not the experience for everyone, my recommendation would be to use an independent party for at least your ovulation testing, as they have no personal interest, benefit or gain to make if your female is or isn't ready for breeding.

Chapter 12 - Artificial Insemination summary

During this chapter, we have covered:

- How AI can offer flexibility for both bitch and stud owners when mating.
- Knowing the benchmarks of a good semen collection.
- The best practices, protocol and husbandry for AI success.
- That defined breeding protocols will help manage matings efficiently.

Part 3 - The Mating Summary

You should now fully understand the mating methods and options available and everyone's key roles. Having an awareness of the complexities that may develop (and how they can be efficiently managed) should result in safe, stress-free and successful matings.

If you need third party assistance, find them in advance and build the rapport to have a robust and reliable relationship. Find out how they like to operate and the best ways to contact them.

Have a clear 'Day 1' of season protocol, so expectations of all parties are effectively managed and communication is kept open and transparent.

Want more help?

Every dog you own is different because they are individuals with their own personalities and quirks. This is no different when you're mating dogs. Until you get the two dogs together, you are never really sure how it will go and whether it will end in success. It's hard to deal with difficult situations when you don't have immediate access to experts or a skilled professional. This book is just an introduction to the minefield of dog matings. Do you:

- Seek more practical advice to handle dogs better yourself?
- Wish to gain confidence in using newer breeding methods and options to help fast track your breeding program
- Want to improve your existing skillset, so you can manage your own dogs more efficiently with added flexibility.

Then the Home Breeder Hub may be for you.

Whether you are the owner of the bitch or stud, the hub can help you make matings streamlined and stress-free. In the Hub, we can plan for the most challenging of matings to ensure the best success. Tap in and use the vital information in the Hub to help give all your planned breedings the best likelihood of success.

Home Breeder Hub - Very Important Breeder (ViB) Access

The Home Breeder Hub is a paid monthly membership for the conscientious dog owner, who I like to call ViB's, Very Important Breeders. This is a fabulous community of breeders who want to raise the bar and seek reliable support and advice. The Hub is the only way you'll have direct access to me, so I can support you on your breeding journey and experiences. If you are dedicated to investing in this pastime, then the Hub is the place for you.

What do you get as a ViB?

- Fortnightly online breeding support sessions offering an opportunity for you to discuss your dog's specific breeding needs and issues - ***Value £197***
- Monthly breeding educational webinar including guest speakers - ***Value £97***
- Quarterly printed and posted publication straight to your letterbox - ***Value £97***
- Unlimited access to all resources within the Hub - ***Priceless!***
- Access to the community forum for more in-depth doggy discussions - ***Value £97***

Book reader offer for you

You can register for the Home Breeder Hub and claim your first month for just **£9.99** by going to **www.caninefamilyplanner.com/DSVIB**

CHAPTER 13

What Next?

That's it, I've imparted as much relevant knowledge and information as I can. What you do with it is down to you. I've tried to share the issues, challenges, and solutions that most owners come up against in their breeding journey. It's the truthful reality of breeding, not a textbook perfect version.

I always tell myself that anyone can own a dog. All types of people walk this earth, so if you can find dog owners with similar views, values, and opinions, it should be a sound foundation for a good relationship that you can both benefit from.

"To learn and not to do is really not to learn."
Stephen R. Covey

It's been a bumpy ride, and this book is jam-packed full of gems. It would be a total waste of your time to have read this book and then decide not to act on any relevant advice or information. You might as well have not bothered reading the book and gained a few more hours watching Eastenders or Corrie.

So please, health test your dogs, research your studs, sign the paperwork, have a firm breeding protocol, and pick the most suitable breeding methods. All these actions will ensure you have a safe, successful and stress-free dog breeding experience.

Once the female has been bred, it's best to try and forget about it until she is ultrasound pregnancy scanned at 28 days from last breeding. Any female that has been covered should be ultrasound scanned; this is an opportunity to check on her health status and development. I cover 'why' in detail in my other book, **Not Born Yesterday**. If you haven't had the chance to read it, I've gifted you a free chapter in this book - Chapter 14 'Pregnancy is a condition, not an illness, or is it?'.

What now?

Once the female is confirmed in pup, you need to read **Not Born Yesterday** in its entirety. It will take you from four weeks gestation until the puppies leave for their new puppy owners' homes at eight weeks.

If the bitch has been confirmed not in pup, once over the initial disappointment, you should start to hatch Plan B. Remember in 'Part 1 - The Bitch' when I asked what type of breeder you are?

"Some owners can't cope with the disappointment, whilst others look at the experience and the financial loss and leave it be, and then you get the people that see it as a personal challenge."

If you feel like it's a personal challenge, then you go again - if you didn't action everything I mentioned in the book, then run through it again and put some of the key points into place. If you followed every instruction to the word, you look at your stud contract and make arrangements for your remate. Then you do it all over again.

Should the bitch miss a second time to the same stud, I recommend you do it again, but use a different stud. There are incidences that two fertile dogs just won't conceive with each other; typically, this is due to their differing internal pH meaning the semen struggles to thrive in her environment.

And, if she still misses, then tell them what I threaten all mine with, to make them into a rug, or if they are too small, a pair of slippers. Obviously, I'm joking.

If they still miss the third attempt, and with two different stud dogs, I strongly recommend finding a veterinary reproduction specialist to further investigate the issue.

The End

So that's it, you've reached the end of Doggy Style, and I'm hoping you felt it was more than worth the read. If you did, please, please, please leave me a 5 star online review wherever you purchased the book or on Amazon. This tiny gesture goes a long way to helping others find this dependable breeding resource.

Though it's the end of this book, it's only the beginning of your breeding journey. If you and your dogs want to live happily ever after, having the best chance of avoiding the most common mistakes and problems, then I recommend you check out the Home Breeders Hub. The Home Breeder Hub is a paid monthly membership for the conscientious dog owners, who I like to call ViB's, Very Important Breeders. This is a fabulous community of breeders who want to raise the bar and seek reliable support and advice. You can register for the Home Breeder Hub and claim your first month for just **£9.99** by going to **www.caninefamilyplanner.com/DSVIB**

I've written this a few times in the book, mainly because I wasn't sure if you would just read the relevant part of the entire book. But it's true, the Hub is the only way you'll have direct access to me, so I can support you on your breeding journey and experiences. If you are dedicated to investing in this pastime, then the Hub is the place for you.

What do you get as a ViB?

- Fortnightly online breeding support sessions offering an opportunity for you to discuss your dog's specific breeding needs and issues - ***Value £197***
- Monthly breeding educational webinars including guest speakers - ***Value £97***
- Quarterly printed and posted publication straight to your letterbox - ***Value £97***
- Unlimited access to all resources within the Hub - ***Priceless!***

- Access to the community forum for more in-depth doggy discussions - ***Value £97***

CHAPTER 14

FREE CHAPTER FROM MY OTHER BOOK 'NOT BORN YESTERDAY'

Pregnancy is a condition, not an illness, or is it?

I can recall my sex education classes whilst in Secondary school. The boys and girls were split into separate classes, and 'the vitals' were explained. Some kids, even-aged 14, could teach more than the teachers. Anyway, the one main takeaway I had from the lesson was:

"If you have unprotected sex and get pregnant, count yourself lucky!"

There was a considerable emphasis on STD's, and you only have to watch 5 minutes of 'Embarrassing Bodies' to put you off your dinner and sex for life.

Like I mentioned before, if your dog could talk, you could give her a real good grilling on what she'd got up to the other night when you came home to find a jailbreak of the cage or baby gate which was safely keeping her and Romeo apart. No doubt she'd be grounded.

Instead, it sometimes comes down to the owners' sixth sense or watchful eye to identify initial signs of possible pregnancy. Observing such changes typically sparks their 'possible' pregnant antenna, suggesting the little pitter-patter of puppy paws may be on the horizon.

So what changes might you see in the early stages of pregnancy, between mating and five weeks gestation?

Before her ultrasound scan for confirmation, I am asked a lot about the signs of pregnancy and whether I could guess if a girl is pregnant.

My answer is always no.

Until the ultrasound probe has made contact with her belly and I see puppies, I never even contemplate trying to guess whether a female is pregnant. I have fallen into previous traps, believing they are or aren't myself for the scan to confirm the opposite.

Signs of pregnancy may include loss of appetite, some females will possibly display morning sickness. This is generally caused by their hormones whizzing around their body, making significant changes to prepare for the pregnancy.

The hormone Progesterone is present after ovulation and is required to maintain a pregnancy. It has been associated with an upset stomach, regardless of confirmed pregnancy. These conditions are also the same symptoms of a dog being ill. If prolonged or in excess; you must seek veterinary advice to identify any underlying problems.

Another common observation is the female becomes attentive and clingy. She always wants to be around people or her preferred owner. She may want her belly to be rubbed or prefer not to have her belly touched. You won't always know whether this is due to pregnancy or pain due to an undiagnosed condition.

She may also become more lethargic, not wanting to get out of her bed, go on her usual walks, or not for as long. A dog looking unwell and not wanting to do its usual routine can also signify illness rather than pregnancy.

Maiden females, who have not previously had a litter, will show little physical indication of pregnancy before 35 days. It's been known for the Oestrogen hormone to aid water retention, which can visually change the shape of your dog. These changes are due to hormones, not pregnancy, around her undercarriage and the vulva (which most pet owners call their foo-foo!).

You may have heard about teats becoming bigger and rosy or changing shape and sagging. These changes can also occur with phantom pregnancies. A phantom is where a female displays all signs of being pregnant, even producing milk, but they're not.

Changing body shape and weight gain could also suggest a possible womb (uterus) infection, such as closed Pyometra. This is caused by the build-up of pus in the uterus, causing her to gain weight and a pregnant 'looking' body shape.

Pyometra could also be the reason for her being lethargic, along with possibly a raised body temperature, panting, loss of appetite and increase in drinking as she's trying to flush her system of the poisons.

Discharge is typical in pregnancy, and a small amount is to be expected, a clear discharge after mating is not a problem. If the discharge is foul-smelling, murky in colour, or could be described as 'strawberry milkshake', this could be open Pyometra. An open uterus infection will have noticeable pus starting to drain from the body.

If you suspect your female may have Pyometra, seek veterinary advice immediately. This is a time-sensitive condition where your female will only deteriorate over time.

Hopefully, I've provided you with enough examples as to why it's so essential to make sure you confirm if your female is in pup. As I learnt from my sex education lesson, pregnancy is most certainly better than an undiagnosed illness.

So what methods are available to confirm pregnancy?

Marred methods to determine motherhood

There are many ways to waste your time and wonga on different techniques wondering if your dog is pregnant. You'll see many 'bright' ideas when researching online.

Method One: Human pregnancy kits

Have you seen the recent craze on social media where the wife or girlfriend reveals to her partner she's pregnant by leaving the pregnancy test kit somewhere for them to find. While the entire revelation is filmed.

I always thought it would be a wicked trick to play on your partner and before they reach new levels of concern say, "ha-ha don't worry it's not mine it's the dog's!" — an easy way to prank them and break the news in an entertaining way that the dog is having a litter.

Well, it wouldn't work, and the prank would be over.

Why?

Because you can't use a human pregnancy kit on dogs. There is a canine version, but it requires a blood draw, not urine.

Most vets won't stock these kits, and more importantly, they can give false-negative results up to 33 days of pregnancy. By then, you can ultrasound scan instead, providing more accurate information.

Method Two: Gums going pale at around 21 days

It's something to do with the blood rushing to the uterus, taking it away from the rest of the body.

I don't believe there's any medical evidence to confirm this is an accurate way of confirming pregnancy. Even if it was, it's not going to give you an idea of the number of pups to expect, or the possible gestational date.

If you take a picture of the gums before and after for comparison, how do you know it's in the same light or at the same angle. With the same period before or after exercise or food - speeding up her metabolism, increasing body temperature, and making it easy to misjudge the colour change.

Method Three: Nip pics

You'll see this plastered all over social media with comments like "Does my dog look pregnant?"

Who knows? Because who knows what they looked like beforehand, Karen?

Old school methodology is teats will become more pronounced and rosy pink. This will be more difficult to ascertain on a female who undergoes these changes but is having a phantom pregnancy or in long-haired breeds.

I'm going to group palpation here too. Generally only advised if a trained person practises it. Which means a vet, feeling around the abdomen. I feel there is little accuracy, even if they are reasonably confident she is pregnant, as the numbers are a total guesstimate.

Method Four: Human foetal heartbeat Doppler

This equipment amplifies the sound of a potential puppy's heartbeat for you to ascertain whether she's in pup or not.

The problem with this is the quality of the equipment, the quality of gel, and the person's skill. You'll find it's hard not to pick up the mother's circulation, picking up her heartbeat through various arteries running through her body. You'll hear a lot of swishing and white noise, which can be misread as puppy heartbeats.

I had a client use this equipment in the later stages of pregnancy when the pregnancy had already been confirmed by other methods. They were panicking because they couldn't find any puppy heartbeats and were concerned they may have died. On further investigation with ultrasound, they were all very much alive, causing unnecessary owner distress.

Foetal heartbeat monitors are in the same bag as the Draminski pregnancy detectors. I believe they run on the same kind of principle. If you don't know what this device is, you don't need to find out due to poor reliability or accuracy.

Don't bother wasting your wonga or time on human pregnancy products or even substandard dog ones.

Accurate Pregnancy Confirmation

You can use ultrasound scanning from as early as 28 days from the last mating, if the person conducting the scan is experienced. This doesn't necessarily mean a vet. A skilled technician will be able to provide you with accurate information about pregnancy and puppy development. To know if they are skilled, ask when booking if they can:

- Identify the correct size for gestation?
- Identify if the puppies have the correct development points?
- Confirm how many puppies they have seen?
- Advise on other general observations?

Later gestational scans can define organs, observe limb movement, and the skull and body can be measured for size and estimate due date.

It is possible to confirm the gestational status of the puppies and the number of puppies expected. The more skilled the technician, the more confident they will be in providing numbers.

Nothing is 100% in life, apart from death and taxes, but scanning will give you a damn good idea of what's going on and help you plan. It will also rule out phantom pregnancies that can give many similar signs and indications as pregnancy, and pyometra, which can be triggered by a season.

Scanning can also pick up things which are not necessarily problematic but untypical, such as empty gestational sacs or the absorption of puppies.

All of this can also be offered in the comfort of your own home. There has been a recent boom in mobile breeder services and fertility clinics assisting at your convenience and ease. These individuals should be highly skilled, experienced, and insured in all their services. If in doubt, check by seeking other breeders' opinions or reviews.

Small businesses offering pregnancy scanning are more likely than your local veterinary branch to have newer equipment and the confidence due to conduct these scans frequently.

A skilled, trained eye may also discover other underlying health issues. The professional won't be able to diagnose but will refer you to your vet. I've found bladder crystals, unusual artefacts such as cysts and masses, pelvic kidneys and closed Pyometra.

I want to mention X-raying quickly. This method is common in America, where ultrasound scanning is highly underutilised. X-raying can only be carried out in the latter stages of pregnancy when the puppies' bones have formed. During this time, ultrasound scanning would have provided similar information sooner without the x-ray emissions. For this reason, they probably should be avoided to prevent any damage to the development of a foetus.

I always liken breeding to gathering parts of a jigsaw puzzle. The more pieces you collect, the clearer the picture becomes.

Confirmation of pregnancy is just one part of the puzzle. There are many more pieces to find during the whole experience.

The next chapter of **Not Born Yesterday** will provide you with a few more puzzle pieces to ensure you and your dog bloom during her pregnancy.

ABOUT THE AUTHOR

Sara Lamont is the world's first Canine Family Planner™, and the leading authority on home breeding. She is passionate about helping pet owners and breeders make the best choice through education, advice and assistance.

Having bred her first litter aged 17, she now has over two decades of experience and has been challenged by the most complex of canine pregnancies and problematic puppies. Sara is a well-respected breeder and international canine conformation judge and has achieved esteemed accolades, including breeding a Crufts 'Best of Breed' winner.

Her company, HomeScan Breeder Services, was launched in 2014, and she now spreads her message of positive planning by educating owners on their litters. Publishing her first book 'Not Born Yesterday' in 2019, launched with its sister workbook 'The Home Breeders Puppy Playbook', the trilogy is now completed with Doggy Style (2022).

In my words …

Let me take a quick minute to explain a little about myself. I'm going to be frank, I'm one of the crazy dog people you see memes about. "If she owns multiple dogs and works with dogs, then run - far and fast.", I'm not going to lie, I never really planned any of this, it just kind of happened.

My mother was firm but fair but never hindered my or my brother's thoughts, ideas or dreams. She believes that if you can think about it, you can do it. She never batted an eyelid when I said I would give up nearly 10 years of corporate Learning and Development consultancy career to become a 'pet scanner'.

She has witnessed decades of blood, sweat, and tears I had put into training and showing dogs, then breeding and bettering them. This is one reason why I have a passion for helping others, well, that and the fact I'm an Aquarius. Yeah, I do believe in some of that shit, and Aqua's are the humanitarian of the Zodiac. Who are revolutionary thinkers that change the world through social progression. Paired with the world now being in the 'age of Aquarius', which started in March 2021 and was set to last a fair while, layered with a 'big' birthday was fast approaching, I felt it was time.

Having published my first book in 2019, it was an enormous sense of achievement to have a brightly coloured, perfectly bound, glossy covered document with some of my organised thoughts and opinions on breeding. By publishing 'Doggy Style', I'm either a glutton for punishment, crazy, or just stepping into my 'calling'.

I'll let you decide.

If you agree, please leave a 5-star review from wherever you bought this book (or Amazon). I can't explain how much that means to me.

Thanks for now.

Sara x

More info: www.caninefamilyplanner.com
Insta: www.instagram.com/caninefamilyplanner
FB: www.facebook.com/caninefamilyplanner

ACKNOWLEDGEMENTS

I felt it only right to give some back story, acknowledgement and thanks to some of the stories I've mentioned in this book and pivotal people in my career and life.

My mum, **Jackie Deen** - If she hadn't given birth to me when she did, you wouldn't have this book in your hand now. It's that simple.

Isobel May-Smith - Mum to smooth mini Dachshunds Indy and son Phoenix, way more than my PA and office angel. We are two Aquariuses plotting world domination daily. I'm blessed we crossed paths and hope for much success for both of us.

Jodi & Steve Bragger (Northwest Breeding Services™) - Jo's my most prominent book advocate. She's sold more of Not Born Yesterday than I care to count, and the Mac Makeup story in that book was for her and Steve's wedding. English Bulldog Breeder, friends, before working peers who come with a 10/10 recommendation from me.

Big dog walk story - **Charlotte & Paul Rose** (Dollondak Dogs) **,** we first met when I handled an English Bulldog stud dog that Charlotte used. Further down the line, she used my dogs in her program. Now, bizarrely (I may have talked them into it), we both own Labradors. The Rose family are crazy, eccentric, non-filtered and funny, just my type of people.

3am Breeding story - **Zil and Kerry** (Loudpack French Bulldogs), we've moved further from each other, yet I always get the blame for it. I'd rarely see Zil in daylight, but we've stayed good friends and catch up on dogs regularly.

Crufts BIS Birthday story - **Margriet Metsemakers** (Temple of Dreams - Netherlands), she's possibly more obsessed with my dogs than I am. She's feisty, fearless but friendly, we've dog holidayed together and had many laughs, and I hope it continues.

Childhood Twin Mum story - **Laurie Franklin-Johnson**, was gassed when I wrote my first book, so I felt she needed a mention in the second. The twins have now turned 18!

Pizza Party story - It was judge **Kelly Wells** (Linmist Bulldogs) that requested pizza. We had the most fabulous trip to Italy together. I look forward to having an equal amount of laughs on any other joint appointments.

Dominic Hodgson - The UK's Leading Pet Business Coach and my mentor. He still very much supports me in developing, building and fine-tuning my business. Constantly pushes his mentees to achieve, despite a pandemic.

And finally, to everyone that bought and read **Not Born Yesterday**. You'll already know that it covers everything from the point of a positive pregnancy confirmation up to when the puppies leave for their new homes at 8 weeks old, basically where this book ends. Both books together, cover in detail the entire breeding journey. So thanks for coming back for the prequel to increase your dog breeding knowledge. I can't tell you the effort that goes into writing a book, so when people buy, enjoy, and learn from it, it certainly makes you feel that writing another is possible. And that I did.

If I've forgotten anyone I should have mentioned, I'm sorry!

Remind me when I write the next.

Printed in Great Britain
by Amazon

80498672R10113